"You can knit better"

Marcia Lynn®

PRESENTS

"You can knit better"

more than *100* ways to improve your knitting

by Lois Larkin

C. J. BATES & SON ● **CHESTER, CONN. 06412**

Art work by
JOHN WESTLAKE
and
CHRISTIANE MARSZALEK

© LOIS LARKIN 1967

CONTENTS

FOREWORD

This book has been written with three things in mind: WHAT, HOW and WHY. *What* and *how* are, of course, extremely important, but they are relatively useless unless the *why* is given.

Using these three words gives meaning to the following tips, and these tips will be valid as long as there are knitters to use needles and yarn. This is not an instruction book and it does not attempt to teach the basic fundamentals of knitting. Its sole purpose is to help the knitter understand more clearly the instruction and direction books and to make the application of these instructions to the knitting easier to interpret.

Many words have been capitalized and underlined. The reader may think that too many words and phrases have been repeated excessively. This emphasis and re-emphasis has been deliberate and the repetition intentional, and for one reason: developing good knitting habits results in a better finished product and there is nothing in the world which can take the place of accomplishment and pride in a job well done.

Lois Larkin

MARCIA LYNN KNITTING BOOK   *by Lois Larkin*

EQUIPMENT

Knitting one article or garment takes only a very few tools; the specified requirements may suffice for your first venture. Your supply of equipment, however, will grow to larger proportions as you progress to new and different accomplishments and, as for any type of endeavor, it must be of the best possible design and construction—otherwise, even the finest work will fall far from perfection. These tools are made in various materials and for special purposes, so that you may choose the type you prefer for the work you have planned.

To avoid any difficulty in knitting, it is advisable to have your knitting needles light in weight, well balanced, and sufficiently flexible to ensure many pleasant hours of work.

KNITTING NEEDLES

If you wish a firm needle which will not break under ordinary pressure, there is the aluminum alloy type which is strong, slightly flexible, and just slippery enough to ensure quick knitting. A more flexible needle is made of plastic which has strength and durability. Both of these materials are made in a choice of colors, which you will find most useful; it is less confusing to knit one color of yarn with a contrasting color of needle—the stitches on the needle are more easily defined when there is this difference in color.

Knitting needles are made in single-point, double-point and circular types.

Single-Pointed Needles are sometimes referred to as STRAIGHT needles and are used for any back-and-forth knitting.

Double-Pointed Needles, often referred to as SOCK needles, are also recommended whenever seams would detract from the appearance and fit of a garment; also for neckline finishes and countless other purposes. If the number of stitches to be used is greater than those used for socks or stockings, it is advisable to use the 10″ length; these longer needles will accommodate more stitches without their dropping off.

Circular Needles are used for many different types of work. The shortest length (16″) is almost indispensable for working ribbing at a V-neckline and for small garments; it might even be responsible for the revival of "Thread Lace Knitting" which advanced knitters find so fascinating. The longer lengths (24″, 29″ and 36″), are used in making sweaters, coats, skirts and dresses. They are absolutely necessary when making a raglan-sleeved sweater which is worked down from the neckline, or for completing a circular yoke. The smaller sizes (generally from #0 through #2) have working tips of aluminum alloy with a connecting portion of nylon. The larger sizes are of all-nylon construction and are used for heavier yarns, including the newest bulky types.

SIZES AND LENGTHS AVAILABLE IN KNITTING NEEDLES

MATERIALS	SINGLE POINTS		DOUBLE POINTS	
	LENGTHS	SIZES	LENGTHS	SIZES
Aluminum Type	10–inch	1–15	7–inch	1–8
	14–inch	1–15	10–inch	1–8
Plastic Type	10–inch	6–15	10–inch	9, 10,
	14–inch	6–15		10½
		17, 19,		
		35, 50		

CIRCULAR NEEDLES	
LENGTHS	SIZES
16–inch	1–10½
24–inch	1–10½
29–inch	1–15
36–inch	5–15

When you have completed the pieces of a knitted article or garment, you will very soon find that knitting needles alone will not be adequate for the finishing. You will find that a crochet hook is almost indispensable for joining seams, picking up "dropped" stitches, or working a crocheted border on a cardigan.

The following list of crochet hooks by no means includes all of the sizes available but, as this is a *knitting* guide, only those are given which you may need for the work to be encountered.

CROCHET HOOKS

MATERIALS	SIZES	TYPE OF YARN USED IN KNITTING
Steel	3–7	Lightweight yarns; bouclé, nubby yarns.
	00–3	Medium- to heavier-weight yarns.
Aluminum or Plastic	B–C	Lightweight to medium-weight yarns.
	D–E–F–G–7– H–I–J–K	Medium- to heavy- to bulkyweight yarns.

ACCESSORIES

As useful aids in the course of the knitting itself, and also for the final finishing and proper fit of garments, there are several knitting accessories which are not only helpful, but actually indispensable; no well-equipped knitting bag should be without them.

Yarn Needles. These come in steel or plastic and in various sizes and lengths to suit the uses to which they will be put. They are used for sewing seams, embroidering in wool, grafting, and countless other purposes.

Knit Count. One size will fit a needle from size 0 thru size 8. A variation of this size includes a built in 8-inch tape measure for measuring as you count. Another larger one will fit from size 9 through size 15. These Knit Counts are especially designed so that you can count the rows and stitches as you work them and are excellent when making cables.

Stitch Holders. For holding stitches securely when not in use, these are available in aluminum or steel, and from 1¾″ to 6¼″ in length.

Cablestitch Holders. These are made of aluminum in various sizes and shapes so that they may best suit the stitches they are to hold.

Yarn Bobs. For multi-color knitting and argyle socks, these also come in a variety of shapes and sizes. They allow the yarn to unwind as needed, and lock and unlock the yarn easily. The regular sizes are usually available in packages of ten. The jumbo sizes come two to a package.

Ring Markers. (Sometimes called Stitch Count Markers). These little markers come in small plastic re-usable boxes containing from 15 to 20 small-to-jumbo sized colored plastic rings. They are slipped onto the needle to designate separate sections of work where patterns begin and end, or where increases or decreases are to be made. They are invaluable when making skirts or sweaters where counting stitches on every round or row would be difficult and tedious, and a *must* for marking the beginnings and ends of rounds or patterns.

Stitch 'N Needle Gauge. This is designed to check stitch and row gauge easily and accurately. The importance of doing this cannot possibly be overemphasized. For details on the proper way to check *your* gauge, see Tip #19. It is also used to check the size of unmarked needles and aluminum (not steel) crochet hooks, as it shows the accurate *Standard* sizes called for in most instructions.

(2)   ADDITIONAL EQUIPMENT

Before any emergency arises, it would be wise to include the following items of equipment:

Tape Measure (of course!)
Scissors (kept in a case for safety)
Transparent 6–inch ruler
Nail File and emery board (for catchy fingernails)
Notebook and pencil

As small items in your knitting bag are easily misplaced or lost, it is wise to keep them all together and readily available in a small case, box, or envelope which should measure at least 6½″ by 4″ and have some good means of fastening it securely. Keep your tape measure, ruler, Stitch 'N Needle Gauge, scissors, sewing needles etc. in it. If the case is made of transparent plastic, each item can be found immediately.

(3)   RESTORING FAMILY TREASURES

Many knitters cling to the needles left to them by their parents or grandparents. As synthetic materials were not known until very recently, they were made of steel, bone, or wood. The bone needles, unless handled with great care, will finally break. The steel needles, unless properly nickel-plated, develop rust spots which should be dissolved and polished off before using. If you do have these keepsakes in fairly good condition and wish to prolong their life, put them in a long stoppered bottle with a few camphor crystals wrapped in a small piece of cloth. You may find that some have developed a whitish coating. Wash them with a mild detergent and dry thoroughly. Apply a little liquid or paste wax and polish with a soft cloth or paper towel.

You may also have some old wooden needles with rough or catchy spots. Using the very finest grade of sandpaper, rub them lightly. Then, using a very slightly dampened cloth dipped in a fine-grade kitchen cleanser, rub them with this until smooth. Let dry thoroughly and wipe off. Crumple up a piece of heavy waxed paper and really *scrub* the entire length of the needle until it is well polished.

YOUR NOTEBOOK (4)

Always carry a notebook and pencil in your knitting bag, whether or not you go to a knitting shop for instructions. You may make adjustments in your knitting, forget to bring along the knit-count, or want to do some figuring, all of which require writing, and will keep you informed until you reach home. It is very difficult to remember all of these things unless you write them down! Also, knitting attracts other knitters like a magnet, and many new acquaintances (with their suggestions and fresh ideas) may be acquired. You will find that this notebook serves many very useful purposes.

YARNS (5)

Literally hundreds of new yarns for hand-knitting have appeared on the market in the last decade. The "old standbys" will always continue in constant use, but high styling has been very definitely introduced into this field and made knitting a very exciting and rewarding adventure. There is hardly an up-to-date wardrobe that does not include two, three, or more hand-knit garments.

Knitting yarns are spun from practically all kinds of natural fibers which include silk, cotton, linen, wool and hair. Hair fibers (mohair, camel's hair, cashmere, angora, alpaca, vicuña, etc.) are *classed with,* but are *not wool; the only true wool* is sheep's wool. There are also synthetics of all kinds, with new ones constantly in the process of development, which are spun into knitting yarns or in combination with natural fibers. When spun with "tender" wools and hair fibers, these synthetics lend strength and longer wearing qualities. Some of the very toughest and sturdiest of all wools come from Ireland, Scotland, Greece and the Scandinavian countries. Some are spun with a small amount of "grease" or lanolin left in them to make them water-resistant for sports wear.

We no longer think of knitting in terms of just socks, stockings, shawls, or rugged outdoor garments. Sweaters—of course; but dresses, suits, coats, and hats, made of appropriate types of yarn to suit the time of day, may well constitute an entire wardrobe from morning shopping through the afternoon, cocktail hour and evening, for dining and dancing. Just think what the knit wardrobe does for the traveler. Where lack of weight and minimal professional care are a consideration, they are almost indispensable!

We must also include here the popular ribbons of all types and kinds. The first knitting ribbons appeared in the 1930's in Europe and very soon found their way here. They are used for a wide range of garments—dresses, blouses, suits, coats and even hats—and may be used either alone or in combination with yarns of all descriptions. The widths most commonly found are 3/16 inch and 1/4 inch, and the materials used in their manufacture are usually rayon or silk, or various percentages of each. There is also a wide range of textures, from the heavier weights through the very sheerest, almost transparent, silk organdies. Some of these ribbons, including the organdies, have fine metallic threads woven into them for dressy "after-five" clothes. Also, many of the heavier ribbons, either soft-textured or crisp taffeta-type, are woven with two or more colors to produce "tweed" effects. Each of these has its own special use to produce the desired effect.

It would be impossible to make an all-inclusive chart here to indicate the sizes of needles which should be used for any one type of yarn or ribbon. It is possible that any yarn or ribbon, knitted separately or together, would use an entirely different size of needle to produce a special stitch or effect. There is *only one determining factor* in knitting *any* garment to proper fit; *STITCH GAUGE,* multiplied by *MEASUREMENT.* The very first thing to look for in any instruction is *GAUGE.* This is usually found immediately after the materials to be purchased. *You will find insistence on GAUGE throughout this entire book as it cannot possibly be stressed too strongly nor too often.*

14

BUYING YARNS (6)

When buying yarn for an article or garment, *always* buy enough to ensure its completion. *Never* buy one or two balls or skeins at a time and trust to good fortune that you will find the same dye-lot when going back for more. In nearly every brand of yarn, no two dye-lots are *exactly* the same. Real tragedy may be avoided by checking the dye-lot number of the yarn before leaving the store to make sure it is all the same, as the use of differing dye-lots in a garment will cause a most unsightly streak. Even "stripping" and re-dying a garment in a darker color cannot remove this streak.

It is always wise to purchase *extra* yarn when there is any doubt about the amount needed. If the yarn which is left over has been kept in good condition and you have not kept it too long, most shops will gladly refund the purchase price. Make sure to keep all the wrappers or tags, as well as the receipt of purchase, until the garment is finished. Use your permanent notebook to keep all of this information written down; name of shop, brand and type of yarn, dye-lot number, color number, amount and date purchased and, if the pattern was especially good and you may want to duplicate it in the future, write down the number of the instruction book and page number. If you have had individual instructions, keep these in a loose-leaf notebook, protected with a clear plastic cover, and write the information about the yarn on these pages.

SUBSTITUTING A DIFFERENT YARN (7)

If you wish to make a garment in a different brand of yarn than the one suggested in the pattern book, check the *yardage* of the yarn you wish to buy against the yardage of the yarn recommended in the book. If they compare favorably, you are reasonably safe in purchasing the same amount. Remember, however, that smooth, light-textured yarns have more yardage to the ounce than those of a crinkly or nubby type. It is wiser, therefore, to buy more of this latter variety to make sure of completing the garment.

THOSE CHANGING STYLES! (8)

If you remember the '40's, you will also remember that skirts dropped from three to five inches in length almost overnight! It will be a real economy to buy two to three extra skeins of yarn if you are making a dress or suit. That knee-length skirt may have to be lengthened to the new proportions and, if you do not have extra yarn of the same dye-lot, it will have to be put away for that mythical "seven-year" period when styles supposedly change back.

When you send the garment to be cleaned, send the extra yarn too. Wrap each skein (minus the paper lable), in a small cotton or mesh bag and have *it* cleaned at the same time. Of course it may not be soiled, but the cleaning will keep it the same color as the garment and there will be no line of demarcation if it has to be used in the future. If you have to wash the garment, wash the yarn too, following instructions in Tip #72.

(9) *TIPS ON WINDING YARN*

When winding a ball from a hank of yarn, always wind it loosely. The life and stretch of the original yarn can be seriously impaired if it is wound too tightly. To keep a ball of yarn from rolling around loose while knitting, wind it so that the working strand may be pulled from the *center* as follows:

Take a small tube (a soda straw, cut to about 4" will do very nicely), run one end through this and wind the yarn around the fingers and thumb, *and* around the tube as well, leaving about 3" of the starting end clutched in your hand and always visible. After about twenty turns, take out the fingers and thumb; still holding onto the starting end, change position of the fingers and start winding again in another direction. When the ball has been wound, tuck the last end under a few strands of the outside of the ball, remove the tube and you're off and running.

(10) *PROTECTING THE YARN*

Always keep the ball of yarn you are working with in a small plastic bag, even if it is a dark color. Light colors, of course, will soil easily, especially if it takes a long time to finish a skein. But dark yarn, if kept in the cover, will have less chance of picking up threads or lint. When using more than one color of yarn, keep each color in a separate small bag unless, of course, you are working a pattern which requires bobbins.

(11) *TRY OUT NEW COMBINATIONS*

If the instruction book calls for a certain kind of yarn, and you would much prefer to play around with a mixture of brands or textures other than those suggested, don't be timid about trying something new and of your own invention. Try out different stitches, color combinations, texture effects. The only cardinal rules in making *any* knitted garment are *good taste, exact measurements* and, again, *GAUGE.*

RE-USING RIPPED YARN (12)

Yarn that has been knitted is very crinkly and will need to be washed before re-using. Rip it out and, as you do, wind it into very loose skeins, wrapping it around a large object such as a box, a large piece of cardboard, or something similar. Tie the starting end to the last end and slip it off, then tie the resulting skein in two or three places, *loosely.* Do not wind too much of the yarn into one skein. Wash and rinse the yarn thoroughly and press out all of the water possible while it is still in the basin. Then, place in a terry cloth towel and wring the towel, with the yarn in it, to get as much more of the moisture removed as you can. Place it on another dry towel and put this, with the yarn lying lightly upon it, on a screen or across two towel racks where the air can circulate all around it. Fluff up the yarn once or twice as it is drying to remove more of the crinkles and retain the "loft."

ABBREVIATIONS (13)

Every knitting book or set of instructions *should* carry an explanation of the different abbreviations and terms used. The following are included "just in case":

K	—Knit
P	—Purl
st (s)	—stitch (es)
tog	—together (as in Knit 2 tog)
sl	—slip (a stitch)
K-wise	—sl a st as though to knit, or insert the needle into the st in a knitting position
P-wise	—sl a st as though to purl, or insert the needle into the st in a purling position
Pat	—pattern
yo—O	—yarn over needle to form a new st. This is done as follows: *Between 2 K sts,* bring yarn forward under right-hand needle and carry it back over the needle.

17

Between 2 P sts, carry yarn back over right-hand needle and bring it forward under the needle.

After a K st and before a P st, bring yarn forward under needle, back over needle, then forward under needle again.

After a P st and before a K st, carry yarn back *over* needle.

wl fwd. (British)	—wool forward; same as yo
SKP—Sl 1, K 1, psso —or Sl, K and pass	—sl 1 st, K 1 st and pass the slipped st over the knit st
dec	—decrease (either K 2 tog or SKP)
inc	—increase
beg	—beginning (of the row or round)
rnd	—round (in circular knitting)
Dp—dp	—double-pointed (needles)
Sp—sp	—single-pointed (needles) ; in crocheting—space
rep—rpt	—repeat
work even	—continue to work as before without increasing or decreasing
sl st	—slip-stitch (in crochet)
sc	—single crochet (stitch)
ch	—chain (crochet)
″	—inch

(14)   *THE ASTERISK*

When reading practically *any* pattern stitch, you are certain to find an asterisk (*): you will invariably find another * towards the end of the sentence. These * * indicate that something in that pattern stitch must be repeated. They are placed there so that part of the instructions, *and only that part between the two asterisks,* not the stitches which are written before or after them, are to be repeated. In the following, you will find an example of a pattern stitch which includes the asterisks:

P 1, * P 1, K 2, P 1, K 4; rep from *, ending P 1, K 2, P 2.

How to work it? Purl the first st *one time only* to start; then, * P 1 (again), K 2, P 1, K 4—and rep just this P 1, K 2, P 1, K 4 to the end of the row where you will find that you have only 5 sts remaining. As these 5 sts are not sufficient to work the 8 sts between the two * *, you therefore work the remaining 5 sts after the last *, which would be P 1, K 2, P 2.

PATTERN MULTIPLES (15)

Every pattern stitch is worked with a definite number of sts. This number is called the *multiple* of the sts used. Some instructions give you this multiple, but others do not. To obtain this multiple, count the number of sts between the two * * as your *multiple* and then add the sts before and after these * * which will make up the *additional* (or *plus*) sts. Reading the instructions for the pattern stitch in Tip #14, the *multiple* would be 8 sts, and the *one st before, plus the 5 sts after* the multiple would be the *additional* or *plus* sts which count to 6. Therefore, the pattern stitch would read: "Multiple of 8 sts plus 6." There *are* some pattern stitches, however, which will accumulate more and more sts during the progress of the work between the first row and the last row. The total number of sts, however, will return to the original count on the last row, leaving you with the initial number of sts when the pattern starts on the first row again.

SIZES (16)

When consulting a knitting or instruction book, bear in mind that the size dress, bra or slip you wear does not, *in any way,* indicate the size of a hand-knitted garment. The size should be based on *your own personal measurements.* The chart gives the *knitted* measurements *usually* planned in the directions.

The measurements given here should not be compared with the size you would buy in a machine-knitted sweater or dress. They are only a guide to help you choose the size of the *hand*-knitted garment that will fit the best. You should, first of all, take the bust measurement. Compare this with the chart and then make the necessary alterations in length and width of each separate piece.

Please bear in mind that these measurements are only those which are most widely used and accepted, and that they may not apply to *your* figure (or the figure of anyone you might be knitting for) in more than one or two dimensions. We are all familiar with the *short-waisted* or *long-waisted* figure, where *half-size* or *tall-size* patterns pertain in ready-made garments. Sleeve lengths vary to a marked degree, especially for someone who is short or tall. Skirt lengths differ for the same reason, as well as shoulder widths and armhole depths. The chart outlined here is only a guide. You must *take measurements carefully* for the proper fit of the garment you are going to make and all work should be planned to coincide with them.

AVERAGE KNITTING MEASUREMENTS (in inches)

	SIZE	CHEST OR BUST	WAIST	HIPS	UPPER ARM	ARM-HOLE	SLEEVE LENGTH
Infants	newborn	18			5½	3	5
	6 mo.	19			6½	3¼	6
	1 yr.	20			7	3½	7
	18 mo.	21			7¼	3¾	8
Children	2	22			7½	4	8½
	3	23			8	4¼	9½
	4	24			8½	4½	10½
	6	26			9	5	12
	8	28			10	6	13½
	10	30			11	6½	15
	12	32			12	7	16½
Women	10	32	24	34	12½	7¼	16½
	12	34	26	36	13	7½	16¾
	14	36	28	38	13½	7¾	17
	16	38	30	40	14	8	17¼
	18	40	32	42	14½	8¼	17½
	20	42	34	44	15	8½	17½
Men	36	36–38			16	9	18½
	38	38–40			16¼	9¼	18¾
	40	40–42			16½	9½	19
	42	42–44			16¾	9¾	19¼
	44	44–46			17	10	19½
	46	46–48			17¼	10¼	20

Select the *width* which will fit. Refer to the blocking measurements whenever these are given, or figure the width by *dividing the number of stitches* for each size *by the gauge*. You can change the *length* of any section without too much trouble; increase or decrease rows may have to be spaced closer together for a shorter piece, or farther apart for greater length. Adjustments in width are possible for stockinette stitch (K 1 row, P 1 row) and simple patterns with a multiple of 2 or 3 stitches, but when there is a pattern with a multiple that would measure more than 1" (for instance, a *multiple* of 8 sts plus 4 and a *gauge* of 3½ sts per inch), it would be better to select another style than to try to make your own changes.

It is always preferable to select a size slightly wider than one which will be even a little tight; there is no law against taking in a seam. You can even make the back one size and the front one size larger, taking in the extra width on the shoulders with a dart. For a dress or suit, you can use one size for the skirt and a different size for the bodice or jacket.

HOW TO TAKE MEASUREMENTS (17)

Bust Measurement (Women) : measure around the fullest part of the bust, holding the tape measure up very slightly in the back. Measure across the back from side seam to side seam as well.

Chest Measurement (Men and Children) : with the chest fully expanded, measure around the fullest part of the chest.

Armhole: measure from the *top* of the shoulder bone, *straight down* to one inch below the armpit. Measure this *straight down; do not curve in.*

Underarm to Waist: at the side seam, measure from the underarm, about one inch below armpit to the *exact* waistline.

Neck to Shoulder: from side of neck to *top* of shoulder bone.

Shoulder to Waist in Front (for a full bust) : measure from the center of the Neck-to-Shoulder distance, down across the fullest part of the bust to the *exact* waistline. This may be a slightly diagonal line.

Neck to Waist in Back: measure straight down from the prominent neck bone at top of spine, to the *exact* waistline.

Sleeve Length: measure from about one inch below the armpit straight down inside of the arm to the wrist bone. This measurement is for long sleeves only. Measure other desired lengths accordingly.

Arm: measure the upper arm, forearm, wrist. Take the wrist measurement exactly, the other two rather loosely.

Shoulder to Shoulder in Back: from the *top, not the side,* of the shoulder bone on one side to the same point on the other side.

Length of Skirt: hold tape at the *exact* waistline. Measure from this point, down the side of the figure, to the desired length.

If the figure is large, or the seat is prominent, measure from the *waistline at front* to the bottom edge, and from the *waistline in back* as well. These two measurements will differ considerably.

Hip: measure the *very largest part of the seat below the waistline.* For a full figure, take the largest measurement when seated. Then, measure from the waistline to this part of the hip.

Shoulder to Waist in Front: This measurement is taken because, especially if the bust is full, more length may be required at the side seam of the front than would usually be found in the so-called "average" figure. It is therefore necessary to knit this extra length and then to make a horizontal dart at the side seam, about 1½" down from the armhole, or to ease in this extra length to match the back at the side edge. However, *do not start easing in this fullness* until at least 3" above the waistline.

Neck to the Waist in Back: This measurement should coincide with the side-seam measurement plus the armhole measurement *plus* at least one more inch. As an example, if the side-seam measures 7½" and the armhole measures 8" the measurement from the neck to the waist should be about 16½". *However* if the shoulders are sharply sloped, the distance from the neck to the waist could be even more. Watch this measurement very carefully. There is nothing quite so awkward in appearance, nor so uncomfortable, as a sweater or blouse that "hikes up" at the back.

Length of Skirt: If there is an exaggerated difference between the front and back measurements, there are two rules to follow: (1) If knitting from the bottom edge up, allow for extra length in the back by binding off gradually when the waistline length has been reached; on a circular skirt, bind off half of the number of sts for the front, and then bind off series of sts toward the back on each side to make up the difference in length. On a two-panel skirt, bind off a series of sts at beginning of very row until about one-half the sts are bound off. Then, bind off the remaining sts. (2) If knitting from the top edge down, cast on about one-quarter of the number of sts required for the entire waistline on a circular skirt, or half the sts for a two-panel skirt back section. Then, cast on at each side, gradually, and in series, numbers of sts toward the front, to make up the difference in length.

HIP

Hip: To avoid that "sitting-down" look while standing up—that too tight, cupped-under-at-the-seat effect, the skirt *must* be planned so that the number of sts required at the *fullest part of the seat,* where you have taken measurements, should be *at least* 3 to 4 inches *above that point;* i.e., if the hip measures 38" at 8" down from the waist, you should have that width *3 or 4 inches below the waist.*

THE MOST IMPORTANT FACTOR IN THE FIT OF *ANY* KNITTED GARMENT IS *CORRECT GAUGE* TIMES *CORRECT MEASUREMENT*.

Making the Swatch. The *only* way to determine *your* gauge is to make a swatch (sample of knitting), *using the same stitch, color and kind of yarn* and *the same size needles* you plan to use in the main part of the knitted piece. To get the best gauge, make a piece about 4" square. The number of sts *across* is your *stitch gauge* and the number of rows is your *row gauge.* Do not bind off, but remove the knitting from the needle.

Smooth out the knitting or steam-press it flat without stretching it, and place the Stitch 'N Needle Gauge (Fig. 1) or a small transparent ruler across the center of the work. Count the number of sts in *two full inches.* Half of this number will make up *your gauge* for one inch. The two inches may have an odd number of sts, leaving you with

Fig. 1

a half-stitch to contend with when multiplying. DO NOT UNDERESTIMATE THE VALUE OF THIS HALF STITCH. This little half-stitch is of the utmost importance when multiplying it by the measurement. As an example, if you multiply your waistline (try 30" for a round number), times 7½ sts (if you measured 15 sts in the 2 inches), you get 225 sts. Now multiply 30" by 8 sts (if you measured 16 sts in the 2 inches) and you get 240 sts. The result is a difference of 15 sts—*2 whole inches!* This makes a difference, not only in sts, amount of yarn used and knitting time, but also in the finished size!

Never use a tape-measure to estimate your gauge. *Never* hold up the knitted swatch while you are measuring (the latter also holds true when you are measuring any piece of knitted work while in progress). *Never* work a swatch for another person and *never* let another person work a swatch for you. If you are making a swatch for an instructor or teacher, or for yourself for that matter, don't "fudge" or try to get out of it by saying "I'm an *average* knitter"— (there is *no* such animal). It just won't work!

(20) DETERMINE YOUR ROW GAUGE

Your *row gauge* is more easily observed on Stockinette Stitch (K 1 row, P 1 row) if you turn the work to the wrong (or purled) side (Fig. 2). Each ridge is a row. This determining of rows per inch is

Fig. 2

very useful when working a sleeve cap, decreasing at V-necklines or in counting an exact number of rows on two picees which should exactly match when joining at the edges. In most knitting pattern stitches, *there are more rows per inch than sts per inch.*

(21) NEEDLE SIZES AFFECT GAUGE

In reading the instructions from a book, you will always find not only the GAUGE of sts per inch, but the *suggested size* of needle to make that gauge. You may find, however, that *that size* of needle will not give *you* the required gauge. You may knit more sts to the inch than the pattern calls for. If this is the case, you are knitting more tightly than "average" and should therefore use a *larger size* needle. Conversely, if you are knitting fewer sts to the inch, you should use a *smaller needle size*. Keep changing your needles until your gauge is exactly correct!

PATTERN STITCHES AFFECT GAUGE (22)

If you have made a swatch of Stockinette Stitch and then change your mind and decide on another type of pattern stitch, you *must not use* the Stockinette Stitch swatch for your gauge. You *must* test the stitch you are going to use in the main part of the body of the garment. *This is most important.* Every pattern stitch will vary to a marked degree in stitches-to-the-inch and, therefore, the swatch must be made *in that stitch*. If more than one type of stitch is to be used in the making of the entire piece, *a swatch of each stitch* should be made and the gauge of each determined.

The popular "Aran Isle" sweaters are combinations of many stitches, some of them "pulling in" (cables etc.), or "letting out" (mesh or fish-net stitches). There *are* some types of "fish net" stitches, however, that are even tighter, more "pulled in" than some of the cable stitches. You must be wary of *any* type of stitch if you have not already made its acquaintance.

TAKING A GAUGE ON OPENWORK (23)

If you wish to plan your garment or article using a loose, lacy stitch, it is wise to make a swatch 6 or 8 inches square so that the stretch, both horizontally and vertically, may be taken into account when planning. The swatch should be pressed both sideways and up-and-down to its fullest extent before taking the gauge, so that the finished article will fit when assembled and blocked. Use this pressed swatch when determining stitch and row gauge, and make sure that you take the amount of stretch into consideration when computing the dimensions of each portion to be made.

CORRECTING UNEVEN ROWS (24)

You may be a knitter who finds that there is a marked dissimilarity in tension between the knit and purl row. This lack of uniformity is universal but, if it is very noticeable, you should attempt to keep your tension the same on every row, or try using two sizes of needles, the smaller needle for the looser row and the larger needle for the tighter row.

25

(25) COLOR CAN AFFECT GAUGE

It has been mentioned in Tip #19 that the same *color* of yarn should be used for the swatch to determine gauge. Another color of the very same yarn can cause a decided change in the thickness of the yarn, enough to make a marked difference in the size of the completed garment. This tragic experience has been witnessed when a blouse, made of white boucle, fitted to perfection. The very same yarn, size of needles and pattern were used for another blouse, only *the color was not the same. The second blouse was almost two sizes too large!*

(26) MAINTAINING AN EVEN GAUGE

The smart knitter keeps a constant watch for any change in the gauge of the piece she is knitting, especially if she puts the work away for any length of time. The *tension* (pressure put upon the needles and yarn) will vary with the change in disposition of the knitter. Worry, illness or irritation of any kind will almost invariably tighten the gauge, while the relaxed knitter is more apt to loosen the gauge. It has also been found that the very *speedy knitter* is most likely to be a *loose knitter.*

(27) CASTING ON

Believe it or not, there are *at least* twelve accepted ways of Casting On—probably more. The two methods shown here are the ones most used and are recommended by the author.

Casting on With One Needle: Leave about a yard and a half for each one hundred sts when fine yarn and small needles are used—more for bulkier yarns and larger needles. Hold yarn in the two back fingers of each hand (Fig. 3) the end from the ball in the right hand. With *Right* hand, draw yarn under the left thumb *toward* you, and then *away* from you *over* the thumb (Fig. 4). Then, using the index finger of the Left hand as a hook, lay finger on *top* of yarn and hook the finger toward the crook of the thumb and forefinger; then straighten this finger up (Fig. 5). Use the resulting loop on the left forefinger as a stitch, insert the needle into the *front* of this loop (Fig. 6) as though to knit it, and use the yarn in the right hand for knitting this st onto the right-hand needle. Continue this procedure for the desired number of sts. Casting on in this manner is a deviation from the usual one-needle method which uses the left hand *only* for holding the two lengths of yarn. The extra twist given to the st results

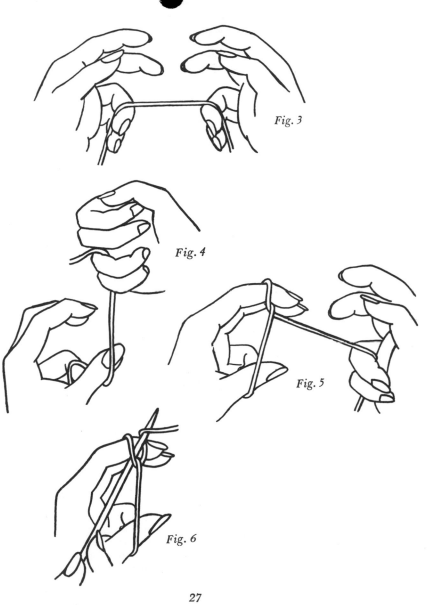

Fig. 3

Fig. 4

Fig. 5

Fig. 6

27

in a firmer, but not tighter, edge at the beginning of the work. Also, when this type of casting-on is used, the first row has already been knitted so that, when working a piece of Stockinette Stitch, it is advisable to start with a Purl row.

(28) *Casting on With Two Needles:* As this does not require two lengths of yarn, it may be started at the beginning of the yarn. Put a slip knot on the left-hand needle (Fig. 7). Holding the yarn in the right hand, knit into the st with the second needle and pull the loop through, but do not remove the original loop from the left-hand needle. Put the loop that you pulled through, back onto the left-hand needle, twisting the right-hand needle so that, when you slip this loop on, the two needle-points are facing in the same direction (Fig. 8). From this point on, instead of knitting *into* this second st on the left-hand needle, as is the ordinary practice when casting on

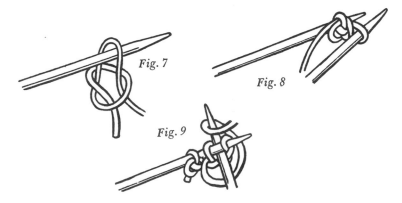

Fig. 7

Fig. 8

Fig. 9

with two needles, insert the needle-point, from front to back, *in between* the two sts on the needle (Fig. 9), wrap yarn around the needle and pull this loop through from *between* the sts, not through the st itself. Twist this loop back onto the left-hand needle. Continue in this manner for the desired number of sts, always pulling up the new st between the last two sts on left-hand needle.

The one-needle method of casting on is used when casting on at the beginning of any one piece. The two-needle method is used when directions indicate the addition of numbers of sts at the beginning of rows during the progress of work, or when replacing the sts bound off for buttonholes and pockets. This does not mean *increas-*

ing, which involves the addition of only *one st* at the edge; it means adding more than one st at any given point.

When working the next row, you will find that there is a very loose, unsightly st which was formed by knitting into the first st of the cast-on group. This hole may be easily closed by working into the *back* of this loose st.

FOR A LOOSER EDGE (29)

Many knitters find that their cast-on or bound-off edge does not "give" as much as it should, which means that it has been put on the needles too tightly or bound off too tightly. To correct this fault, try using a larger needle (or two needles held together) for the cast-on row, and a larger needle for the bound-off row.

COUNTING THE ROWS (30)

Every written instruction involves *numbers of rows.* Whenever the sts have been transferred from the left-hand needle to the right-hand needle, a row has been completed. This is mentioned only because many European directions consider that *once across* the needle *and once back* (especially in Stockinette or Garter Stitch) constitutes "one row." This is not the case in English instructions.

YOUR FIRST PROJECT (31)

One of the best knitted articles for a *beginner* to make is a V-neck sweater. Practically all of the problems that arise in knitting will present themselves at one time or another and must be solved during its making. Working (and "working" is used advisedly) a scarf or some other very simple article is dull and tedious and seldom inspires further effort. On the other hand, a sweater you have made and can wear with pride, provides the incentive to knit many more beautiful additions to your wardrobe. From that point on, the sky is the limit!

HINTS ON RIBBING (32)

For a better seam in K 2, P 2 ribbing, cast on a number of sts divisible by 4, *minus* or *plus* 2 sts. Then, work as follows:
Row 1: * K 2, P 2—rep from * across the row, ending with K 2.
Row 2: * P 2, K 2—rep from * across the row, ending with P 2.

Repeat these 2 rows for the desired amount of ribbing and, when working the last row, inc. (or dec.) 1 st at each end of the needle *if* the pattern of the next row requires 2 sts more or less. When joining the seams, you will find that the ribbing at the edges of the seam will form a complete rib pattern.

When working K 1, P 1 ribbing, cast on an *uneven* number of sts and work the required amount of ribbing, starting and ending the first row with K 1, and starting and ending the second row with P 1. Increase or decrease 1 st on the last row if necessary, to make the required number of sts for the balance of the work.

When working any type of ribbing, make sure to work the same number of rows on each matching piece, and to start the first row of Stockinette Stitch or pattern stitch with a *knit* (or right-side) row unless otherwise specified. This will help to ensure a more uniform joining at the seams.

(33) CONTINENTAL RIBBING

A novel way of working K 1, P 1 ribbing is found in imports from Europe. It has a little more elasticity than the more familiar type and "snaps back" into place better after being laundered or cleaned. It is called "Italian" or "Twisted" ribbing and is worked by knitting into the *back* of each K st on every row. An even more tightly twisted rib may be made by working into the *backs* of *all* sts instead of just the K sts.

(34) CROSS-STITCH RIBBING

This ribbing, as well as the two just described in Tip #33, may be used anywhere, on any sweater or blouse where ribbing is indicated. The multiple (see Tip #15) to be used here is 3 plus 1—13, 25, 34 etc.— and worked as follows:

Row 1: * P 1, skip 1 st and K the 2nd st on Left-hand needle but *do not slip it off*. K the skipped st and *then* remove the 2 sts at the same time. Rep from *, ending P 1.

Row 2: * K 1, P 2—rep from *, ending K 1.

Repeat these 2 rows for the desired amount of ribbing. Buttonholes are easily made in all of these types of ribbing. Just make sure to *bind off in ribbing,* following the directions for making a buttonhole (see Tip #85).

PRACTICING PATTERN STITCHES

Before starting a piece of knitting involving a large number of sts with a new and complicated pattern stitch, make a good-sized swatch of that stitch, casting on the correct multiple (see Tip #19), using large needles and heavy yarn of a light color. It will be very much to your advantage if you become thoroughly acquainted with the appearance of the sts as you work them and to understand how and why they are worked in the sequence indicated in the directions. Then, when working the stitch in finer yarn, there will be much less danger of making mistakes. There is nothing more discouraging than to start a piece of knitting on a large number of sts, and then get all mixed up when only a half-inch or more has been worked. Again, it is stressed, *practice first,* and then go ahead with confidence.

DECREASING

The two most widely accepted ways of decreasing are—K 2 tog—which makes the resulting st slant to the right (Fig. 10) and—SKP (or Sl 1, K 1, psso) —which makes the resulting st slant to the *left* (Fig. 11). In the case of this latter decrease, it is much easier and the result is a tighter and smoother st if you work it as follows: Sl the first st

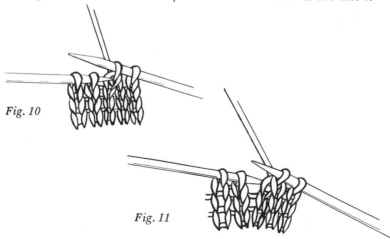

Fig. 10

Fig. 11

from the left-hand needle *knit*-wise and then the second st in the same manner, onto the right-hand needle. Insert just *the very tip* of the left-hand needle into the *fronts* of these 2 sts which are now on the right-hand needle, and knit them together from this changed position.

Using these two kinds of decreases is an *absolute must* when making any "full-fashioned" shaping. They should also be used when making a skirt from the bottom up, using the K 2 tog for one decrease round, and the SKP for the next decrease round. Alternating these two decreases will keep the skirt from pulling slightly on the bias, which may happen when only one kind of decrease is used.

It is also strongly advised to develop the good habit of using these two decreases when shaping armholes and sleeves—*SKP* at the *beginning* of any shaping, and *K 2 tog* at the *end* of any shaping. It is extremely important when shaping the neckline of a V-neck sweater or dress. When decreasing this type of neckline, it is also advisable to make the decreases about 2 or 3 sts *in* from the very edge. In other words, when instructions call for a decrease at the neck edges, work as follows: Work to the last 4 sts, K 2 tog, K 2. At the beginning of the other edge of the V, K 2, SKP, and work to the end of the row as advised in the pattern. These two kinds of decreases will greatly facilitate picking up sts when assembling and finishing, giving you a good, straight edge of knitting that will help you to see where to insert the needle.

(37) DECREASING A PATTERN STITCH

When a complicated pattern stitch is involved, it may prove to be helpful if the decreasing is done on each edge on the *wrong* side of the work. When making the next row, you can see more clearly how to work the pattern.

(38) DOUBLE DECREASES

If you find it necessary to decrease more than one st at a time, the instructions will probably give you the method to use. Just in case they don't, however; for a double decrease work as follows (instead of knitting 3 together) :

Sl 1, K 2 tog, and pass the sl st over the K 2 tog—or—
When taking 4 sts tog:

SKP, K 2 tog, and pass the SKP over the K 2 tog.

DECREASING A SLEEVE CAP

You may find that the sleeve cap, after shaping, turns out to be too small for the armhole.

One of three things may be wrong; first, the armhole itself was measured incorrectly, making it too large for the sleeve to set in properly. Second, the decreases for shaping the cap, or the bound-off sts were worked too tightly. Third, the decreases may have to be spaced farther apart to give the correct number of rows or inches. A sleeve cap should have plenty of "give" so that it will not only fit into the armhole correctly, but also allow plenty of action room for the wearer.

INCREASING

The increase in most common use (many knitters know of no other) is to knit into the front and then into the back of the same st. This method is quite proper when edges of work are to be joined later in a seam; also when the increases are to form part of a pattern on the garment, such as seen in raglan seams, etc.

There is also the yarn-over (yo—or O) which is used deliberately to make an open space, and which also provides an extra st in the work.

There are many times, however, when an increase should *not* be noticeable. On a skirt, blouse or jacket, where increases are made in the body of the work, the following two methods of increasing should be used. Just as in decreasing, increases may be made to slant to the right or to the left.

Knit Increase to the Right (Fig. 12) : Work the number of sts designated, turn your work on the left-hand needle slightly toward you so that you may see the back of the work over the top of the needle. Insert the right-hand needle *downwards* into the little purled bump in back of this st on the left-hand needle and knit this bump as a st; then, work the st on the left-hand needle which is right above this increase.

Knit Increase to the Left (Fig. 13) : Work *every st* to the point where the increase is to be made. Using your left-hand needle, insert it *from the back to the front,* under the last st worked on the right-hand needle *but—one row down. Push back* a little *on just this one thread,* thus making an extra st on the left-hand needle. Knit into the *back* of this st.

33

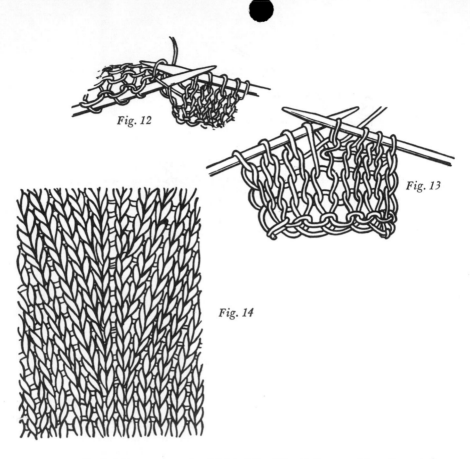

Fig. 12

Fig. 13

Fig. 14

Purled Increase to the Right (Fig. 15) : *Before* working the specified number of purled sts, use the right-hand needle to dip under the
little purled bump *under* the first purled st of the group on the left-
hand needle. Lift this loop up and onto the left-hand needle and
purl it.

Purled Increase to the Left (Fig. 16) : Work to, and including, the
last st of the specified number of purled sts in the pattern or set of sts.
Then, using the tip of the left-hand needle, dip under the little
purled bump just *under* the last st on the right-hand needle. This
will make an extra st on the left-hand needle which should be purled.

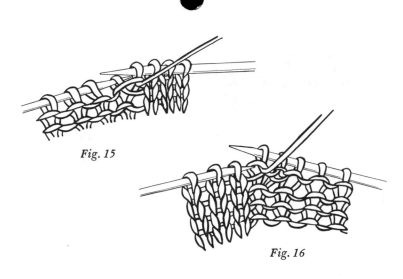

Fig. 15

Fig. 16

In working plain Stockinette Stitch, where increases are certain to show, the common increase (K into the front and back of the same st) should be avoided at all costs and either (or both) of the increases just outlined should be used. We have found it much better to work skirts *from the top down,* thus making any future adjustments in length less complicated. Also, we have found that *decreases,* either to the right or to the left, are more likely to show than the nearly invisible increases described here. In working any kind of pleated skirt, these four types of increases are invaluable.

When using either of the increases—knit or purled—you should increase to the *left* when *approaching* a marker, a set number of sts, or a particular division of the work, and to the *right* when going *away* from the marker or set of sts. (Fig. 14).

Making Increases Across One Row

Many times you will run into the problem of having to increase from a given number of sts in one row to another number of sts in the next row, without the instructions indicating how to space these increases evenly. This problem is easily solved if you follow just this one rule:

Divide the number of sts you have on your needle by the number of increases to be made. Suppose you have 49 sts on your needle and must increase across one row to 67 sts. This means increasing 18 sts.

Divide 49 by 18 which gives $2 + 13$. This means that you must increase in every 2nd st—but—there are 13 sts left over. Divide the remaining number of sts in half and work one half at each end of the row. So—work 7 sts, then increase in each 2nd st 18 times and work the remaining 7 sts.

If you prefer to have the increases more evenly balanced, you may work the problem as follows: * K 1, inc in the next st, K 2, inc in the next st—rep from * across, *omitting* the last increase. In this manner, you would increase 2 sts in every 5 sts and have 18 additional sts.

(41)   *MARKERS—To Mark Rows*

A very simple way to keep track of increase or decrease rows is to work a few sts at the beginning of the row, then (Fig. 17), using a short length of sewing thread of contrasting color, work this in with the knitting for four or five sts, making sure to work both threads off together on the return row. Leave the marker in the knitting until *all* work has been completed; it is easily removed later.

This method of counting rows or rounds is especially useful when two pieces of knitting must exactly match at the edges. It is also valuable when used as a device for measuring vertical distances such as side seams, armholes, etc.

MARKERS—To Divide Stitches

When sts are to be divided into groups across the needle, ring markers should be used. If they are not available, however, use a loop of yarn about 6″ in length, double it and tie a knot at the *end,* not right up against the needle. These markers, when used properly, can save a lot of needless counting of sts or rows. Place marker on the needle at the point specified in the instructions. Then, on every row (Fig. 18), slip the marker from the left-hand needle to the right-hand needle. If using a yarn marker, pass the yarn in *back* of the marker, thus weaving it through the work as you knit; when using a circular needle, pass the yarn in *back* of the marker on the first round and in *front* of it on the next round. Alternate these two rounds to keep the marker running through the work. When the knitting is as long as the marker itself, clip off the knot at the end so that the loop will continue to slip through the work.

(42)   *USE MARKERS BETWEEN PATTERNS*

When working one pattern in conjunction with Stockinette Stitch,

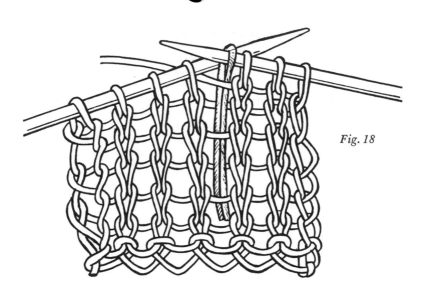

Fig. 18

or different patterns, place a marker between each pattern. This will help to determine where each pattern begins and ends and eliminate counting.

SLIPPING STITCHES (43)

Sts are slipped either *Knit*-wise or *Purl*-wise, and for very important reasons. Unless otherwise indicated in the instructions, a st is slipped *Knit*-wise whenever a *decrease* is made—SKP, sl 1, K 2 tog and psso—etc. These types of decreases are used in lace-making, turning heels of socks, decreasing for toes of socks, beginnings of rows where decreases are in order (see Tip ♯36), etc.

And—unless the instructions indicate otherwise—sts are slipped *Purl*-wise whenever a *pattern stitch* is involved to obtain a fabric appearance. The sts are slipped in this manner so that, on the next row, these sts will be on the needle in the proper position for working.

WHEN TO USE SLIP STITCHES (44)

There are very few instances when *all* sts are not to be worked except, of course, in a pattern stitch where slipped sts *must* be used for a desired effect. In other words, many knitters have been taught to *slip the first st of every row. DON'T,* with the following three exceptions:

1. When an edge, such as the border of a cardigan, is worked in Garter, Seed, or any comparable stitch, used in contrast to Stockinette Stitch in the body of the article. If the knitter finds it difficult to keep the edge firm, the first st *may* be slipped instead of worked, *but*—slipped *knit*-wise. This will help to keep the edge of the work taut and smooth.

2. When decreasing to the *left* as described in Tip #36.

3. When turning on *short rows,* the first st must be slipped.

(45) *JOINING YARN*

Try at all times to avoid tying two pieces of yarn together at any point except at the edges of the work. This is especially true when working with smooth yarns. The ends may be run into the seams when finishing. Crinkly or nubby yarns, however, may be tied at any point in the work with no ill effect. In this case, tie a *square knot* (see "The Boy Scout Manual"—"Left Over Right, Right Over Left") —right up against the needle.

Joining yarn when working a skirt or socks cannot be avoided, so join in the following manner: Overlap the two ends of the yarn about 6″ and knit (or work in pattern) for about 6 to 8 sts with this double yarn. Make sure, however, to work these double sts off together on the next round. Or—just drop the yarn at the end of one ball and pick up a strand of the next ball. Leaving about 4″ of each end just dangling, work several rows or rounds and *then,* snugging up the two threads to the gauge of the knitting, tie them together at this point in a square knot. All of these ends of yarn can easily be threaded into a yarn needle and woven in on the wrong side when finishing. Under no circumstances put two ends of yarn together and tie them in a single knot!

One more thing before leaving this subject: When joining a new length of yarn in a skirt where there is a pattern stitch dividing panels, or a ribbed or pleated skirt, tie in the new yarn where the pattern changes. At finishing time, the ends may be invisibly woven into the work *vertically,* following the line of the pattern or pleat, or *horizontally,* if the pattern runs "sideways", the needle barely skimming the purled knots at the back of the work, for about 4 or 5 sts.

EXCEPTION TO ONE RULE (46)

It is not necessary to weave *all* loose ends of yarn into the underside of a skirt, except toward the bottom edge where one hanging loose might show. Simply cut the loose ends, leaving about 2" and let them hang. Unless the knitting is extremely loose, these ends will not pull through to the right side of the work.

MEASURING WORK CORRECTLY (47)

To Measure Knitting in Progress: With the knitting on the needle, and held to your *left,* lay the work down on a flat surface which will hold the entire piece generously (a large table top or a smooth bed or couch). Using a flexible tape measure (*not* a carpenter's steel tape), place the end of the tape *just under the needle* and measure *down* to the starting point, or to the point which is marked or indicated in the instructions (Fig. 17). Do *not* stretch your knitting; it is hoped that you have determined the amount of stretch when making your swatch. Simply *smooth* your work out as it would naturally lie. Don't cheat by trying to make your knitting measure longer than it really is. You might only have to rip it out and do it over again. On the other hand, try not to be over-generous.

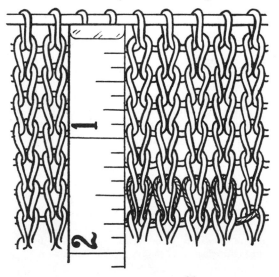

Fig. 17

Never hold work up to measure it! When a garment, such as a skirt or coat, may stretch from the sheer weight of the material itself, stop the knitting at about 2" to 3" of the required length and let it hang for a few days. This time may be shortened if the knitting is left to hang over a bath where there is moisture in the air. Then, measure the knitting again on a flat surface. It has probably stretched considerably. In the final blocking, however, it will stretch a bit more. You must depend on your own good judgment to determine the finished length.

(48) *MEASURING AN ARMHOLE CORRECTLY*

Just as in taking body measurements (Tip #17), the armhole is measured *straight down* from the shoulder, not *curved in*. Nearly all instructions will specify measuring the armhole *straight up from the bound-off sts*. Following Tip #41, work a *horizontal* marker into the knitting, on the same row that the first bind-off is made, about 3" in from the edge of the work. Then, when measuring the armhole, measure from the needle *down* to this marker.

(49) *STITCHES IN MOST GENERAL USE*

Garter Stitch: Knit all sts on every row. When making Garter Stitch in circular knitting, one round should be knitted and the next round purled.
Stockinette Stitch: Knit all sts on one row, and purl all sts on the next row. In circular knitting, *all* sts are knitted on every round.
Seed, Moss, or Rice Stitch: (These are different names for the same stitch.) On every row, each stitch with the *purled* side facing you is *knitted* and each stitch with the *knit* side facing you is *purled*. When working a large piece of Seed Stitch, it is easier to work with an *odd number of sts*. Thus, every row begins and ends with a knit stitch.

(50) *COUNTING CABLE ROWS*

When working cables, unless otherwise specified in the instructions, set your *Knit Count* (see Page 11) to Row 1 on the row *following* a cable twist. This will assure that every odd-numbered row will be on the *wrong* side of the work and every even-numbered row on the *right* side of the work. As nearly every cable is crossed on the right side of the work, and these rows are referred to as every 4th, 6th, 8th row, etc., this method of counting rows makes for less confusion.

HOW TO USE A CABLE-STITCH HOLDER (51)

When working a cable, slip the desired number of sts onto the cable-stitch holder (Fig. 19) and very lightly stick the left-hand point of the holder into the knitting. This will keep it firmly in position and the sts from falling off. Work the specified number of sts from the left-hand needle and then, instead of knitting the sts from the holder (which may be very awkward), slip them back onto the left-hand needle and *then* knit them off from this. You are less likely to misplace or lose the holder if, instead of putting it down, you stick it lightly into the piece of knitting where it will be readily available for the next cable.

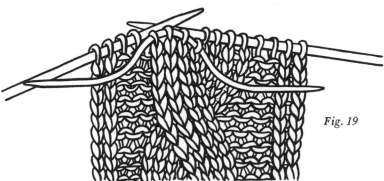

Fig. 19

TO SIMULATE KNITTING IN CROCHET (52)

A belt or strap is often made for a dress, coat, etc. As the knitting itself may not be firm or thick enough, there is a method of crocheting which looks exactly like knitted Stockinette Stitch. It is a variation of *Afghan Stitch* and is worked as follows:

Work with the same size *aluminum* (not steel) hook as the size of the knitting needles used in the garment.

Make a chain of crochet, the desired width of the piece.

Row 1: Draw up a loop through the horizontal bar in back of the second st from hook and each of the remaining sts, keeping all the loops on the hook across the row. There should be the same number of loops on the hook as the number of sts chained.

Row 2: Yarn over the hook and draw it through the first loop on the hook—* yarn over and through 2 loops together—rep from * to the end of the row. There will be 1 st on the hook.

Row 3: The loop that remains on the hook is the first st of this row. * Put the hook *straight through* the next st, *from the front to the back* and pull a loop through. Rep from * across the row. Repeat the 2nd and 3rd rows for the desired length, ending with Row 2. Bind off by slip-stitching across the sts of the last row.

(53) *WORKING A HEM*

There is one cardinal rule to follow when working a hem: Unless the sts (in *any* instructions) are to be increased after the *turning row, the sts of the hem should very definitely be worked on a smaller needle.* It is most urgently suggested that this tip be followed. There is nothing that contributes a more ungainly look to a jacket or skirt than a hem which "pokes out" at the lower edge. The *inside* (turned up portion) of a hem should *always* measure slightly less in width than the body. This will not pucker or gather the work; it will just hold it in the proper position and, when blocked, will keep it in proportion.

(54) *BINDING OFF A SERIES OF STITCHES*

Whenever binding off in a series (shaping shoulders, tops of sleeves, etc.), bind off the first number of sts on each side as usual. Then, on each succeeding bind-off, *slip* the first st, do *not* work it. This will give less of a step-up, more of a straight line.

(55) *BINDING OFF PATTERNS AND RIBBING*

Unless you are working in Stockinette Stitch or Garter Stitch, *never* bind off by knitting every st as you go, unless there is a specific reason for doing so. In other words, if you are knitting a pattern stitch, *always bind off in that same pattern stitch,* whether it is a knit, purl, slip stitch, yo, K 2 tog, etc. This is especially important when binding off ribbing. Each knit st should be knitted and each purl st should be purled, so as to retain the same *ribbed* stretch and appearance throughout. When binding off Garter Stitch, this should be bound by *Knitting* on the *wrong side,* or *Purling* on the *right side.*

BINDING OFF WITH A CROCHET HOOK (56)

If you have a large number of sts to bind off at one time (the bottom of a skirt, for instance), it may prove easier to use a crochet hook as follows: Hold the yarn in the left hand as in crocheting and insert the hook into the first st on the left-hand needle and pull a loop through. Insert the hook into the next st on the needle, draw a loop through this st and *also* through the st on the hook, slipping the st from the needle as you work. Continue in this way until all sts are bound off. Make sure, however, that the bound-off sts are kept to the same tension as the knitting itself.

DIVISION OF NECKLINE (*Back and Front*) (57)

Necklines may be round, square, oval, deeply scooped, V, or what have you. It is much easier and safer to make both halves of one piece at the same time, dividing the work as instructed, and working each half with a separate ball of yarn. Thus, increases, decreases, bind-offs or other kinds of shaping on each half are made simultaneously, with less confusion and the chances of making mistakes kept to a minimum. *However,* never put your work down with only one half completed. Knit at least one inch of sts of the other half because, if you stop at the neck edge, you might easily forget which side to work next!

The same rules apply when making two sleeves or two fronts of a cardigan or jacket. Sleeves are usually made alike with the increases (if necessary) worked at the side edges. It may seem to take a little longer to make two at the same time. However, they both have to be worked, and just think of the relief to know that they are finished when you bind off!

The two fronts of a cardigan or jacket may be worked in the same way, always keeping in mind, however, that any shaping must be reversed. If working with two or more colors however, you may prefer to finish each side separately, but *mark* each increase or decrease row so that both sides will be identical.

(58)　*V-NECKLINE SHAPING*

A *high* V-neckline is usually divided about one inch *above* the shaping of the armhole. A *medium* V-neckline is divided about one inch *below* the armhole shaping, and a *low* neckline is started even lower, depending upon the depth desired. The classic "Tennis Sweater"— usually made with a white cable-stitch body and with navy and red trim—is worked with a very deep V-line and filled in afterward with a wide neckband. When a very deep V with a wide neckband is made, there should be some slightly scooped shaping at the back neckline because, if the ribbing is to be wide enough in the front, the neckline would otherwise be much too high in back. One thing to remember; the *lower* the V-neckline, the *longer* the distance between decrease rows. Use your row-gauge to determine how close together they should be made.

(59)　*PICKING UP STITCHES*

This term, "picking up" sts, is entirely erroneous and is misleading in the extreme to a beginner. It is so generally used, however, that it has become a common expression in all knitting instructions. It is actually a *knitting* operation, *using the needle and yarn* to knit up sts at the edge of the work which has already been knitted. There are many methods of accomplishing this, but only two are generally accepted:

1. Tie in the yarn at the point given in the instructions. Then hold the knitted piece in the left hand, right-side facing you unless otherwise specified. Using the yarn and one needle, insert the point of the needle into the work, *at least two threads (not sts) in* from the edge, wrap the yarn around the needle as in knitting, and pull the loop through to form a st on the right-hand needle.

2. Using a crochet hook, insert the hook into the work as above and pull a loop through. Slip this loop onto the right-hand needle and repeat this operation along the edge of the work, *at least two threads in,* for the desired number of sts. It may be easier, when using a crochet hook, to pull up several loops before slipping them onto the knitting needle. In this case, slip the loops from the *back end* of the hook onto the needle.

There are three main points to remember: Pick up the number of sts given in the instructions or, if no number is given, pick up *to the gauge of the body of the work* (see Tip #19). *Do not get too close to the edge,* and, if you have one handy, use a smaller size needle for the picking-up operation and then work the ribbing or other type of border with the size needle given in the instructions.

SPACING PICKED-UP STITCHES EVENLY (60)

The type of finish will determine the number of sts to be picked up at any given edge. A *shaped* edge will require your close attention, as the decreases or increases may give a little trouble unless they have been made 2 or 3 sts from the edge (see Tip #36). A *straight edge* (as on the front of a cardigan), is much less of a problem, as the needle can find its way into the edge sts very easily. As a general rule, you may determine the number of sts to be picked up in the following manner:

Measure the edge of the work where the sts are to be taken, making sure not to stretch this edge. Multiply the *inches* of the work *times* the number of the sts of the *gauge* used in the body of the garment and use the resulting number obtained for the finishing trim. If there are one or two sts more or less, this will not be over-important, unless a specific multiple is required.

If the border is to be ribbed, you should pick up about *three sts to every four rows* of knitting. This also holds true if the border is *not* ribbed, but if a smaller size needle is used with a different type of stitch in mind. If the border is Garter Stitch, Seed Stitch, or something similar, it is wise to make a small swatch of the type of trim you desire, so you can count the number of sts per inch. It will usually be found, in these instances, that you should pick up *two sts to every three rows* of knitting (Fig. 20). In almost *any* kind of finish, it is far wiser to have the edge a *very little shorter* than the original edge. This can easily be blocked to the distance needed in the final touching up. A "droopy" front edge or loose ribbing on a cardigan or jacket is most unattractive!

STITCHES LEFT ON HOLDERS (61)

Putting sts on holders or threads for future use is often unavoidable, especially when shaping a neckline. Some of these sts may have stretched by the time you do the final finishing. Any unsightly holes may be closed at each end of the "held" sts when picking up sts for the border. Pick up an extra st at each side of these sts and, on the next

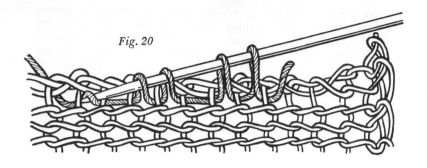

Fig. 20

row, Knit or Purl the extra st together with the one preceding or following it, giving a little extra tug to the st made. This should successfully close the gap.

(62) ### *SHAPING THE NECKLINE*

Many a round-necked sweater is made according to the instructions but fails to slip over the head easily. This is usually the result of having bound off the sts too tightly after the last row of ribbing or finishing. However, some instructions say to bind off sts at the front and back of the neck instead of putting them on a stitch holder, and then, when finishing, pick up the sts across this bound-off edge. This may be perfectly correct if the neck is wide or an opening is provided. With a *pullover,* however, the sts *should* be placed on a holder to give the proper amount of stretch for slipping it over the head.

If your pullover is to have *no* opening and a *high* round neck, it may be wise to shape the *back* of the neck as well as the front. Any shaping at the *front* is usually done *at least two inches* before the shoulder shaping. If you wish to shape the *back* of the neck, it should be done at least *one inch* before the shoulder shaping. Following this procedure will allow you enough room to pick up more sts for the neck-band. Watch out for that final bind-off, however, to make sure that it isn't too tight!

(63) ### *MAKING A NECKBAND FOR A V-NECK*

Join the shoulder seams. Tie in the yarn at the neck edge of the *left* shoulder seam. Using 10-inch DP needles, or a circular needle of the correct size and length, pick up the sts along the edge, following Tips #59 and #60. As the shaping of a V-neck edge *may* produce a few sts on the edge which seem loose, work into a st very near it which is a little tighter, rather than to knit into a loose st and leave an unsightly hole in the finished work. If you have followed Tip #36, this particular problem will not arise. Remember that GETTING TOO CLOSE TO THE EDGE OF THE WORK WHEN PICKING UP STITCHES IS A DEFINITE FAULT.

When all sts have been picked up on this edge of the V, count the number. If a circular needle is used, place a ring marker at this point. Using a second DP needle, pick up the sts along the edge from the V to the right shoulder seam, picking up two more or two less sts if K 2, P 2 ribbing is to be used, than were picked up on the opposite edge. (Pick up one st more or one less if K 1, P 1 ribbing is to be used, and the *same* number if using a circular needle.) With a third DP needle, knit st for st across the back of the neck, adding or subtracting one or two sts if necessary, to make the resulting number of sts divisible by 4 for K 2, P 2 ribbing, or by 2 for K 1, P 1 ribbing. If the sts are picked up in this manner, needles #1 and #3 will start with K 2 or K 1 on *every round,* and end with P 2, or P 1, thus ending properly to start the next needle. If you use a circular needle, the only thing to watch out for is at the *end* of the entire round, where the sts were started. You wouldn't wish to have the proper sequence of ribbing broken at this point, so place a ring marker at the starting point and *make* the sts conform to the ribbing by decreasing or increasing one or two sts at the back of the neck if necessary. If using DP needles, number them as follows:

#1—going *down* to the V from the left shoulder.

#2—going *up* from the V to the right shoulder.

#3—going across the back of the neck (Fig. 21).

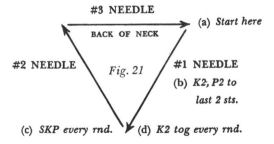

#3 NEEDLE

BACK OF NECK

(a) *Start here*

#2 NEEDLE *Fig. 21* #1 NEEDLE

(b) *K2, P2 to*

last 2 sts.

(c) *SKP every rnd.* (d) *K2 tog every rnd.*

47

On #1 needle, K 2, P 2 or K 1, P 1 to the last 2 sts and, *always, every rnd,* K the last 2 sts tog at this point. At the beginning of the #2 needle, *always, every rnd,* SKP (see Tip #36), pulling the slipped st *very firmly* to prevent making a hole at the point of miter. Proceed in pattern of K 2, P 2 or K 1, P 1—*but start*—after the SKP, *with the same st or sts you ended with* on #1 needle, *just before* the K 2 tog. This will make a symmetrical miter, with the two decreases at either side of the miter in the finished work as two Knit sts (Fig. 22). When using a circular needle, the 2 decreases should be made at the ring marker at the point of the V, following the instructions given for the *end* of #1 needle, and for the *beginning* of #2 needle.

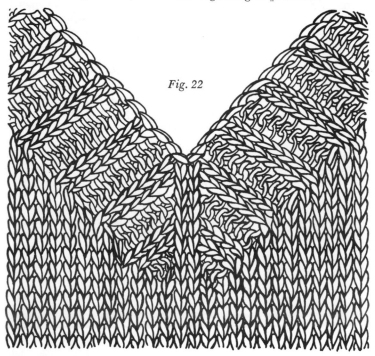

Fig. 22

(64)   *ASSEMBLING THE PIECES*

There are many ways to join the seams of a knitted garment. Although nearly all instructions indicate that a seam should be sewn or

48

grafted at the side edge, we do *not* recommend these methods as being the best except in a few instances which will be described later. There is no great virtue in making a seam as close to the edge as you can possibly get it. In any case, A SEAM SHOULD *NEVER* BE JOINED BY *OVERCASTING* OR BY *SINGLE CROCHET,* except in certain specified instances where the joining will show on the *right* side of the work for a special reason.

Also, a seam may be joined by using a running back stitch, using yarn and sewing needle. If you prefer to use this method, just be careful not to draw the stitches too tight, as any type of joining should have as much give as the knitting itself.

The following method is the one we prefer, as it allows slightly more give than a seam which is sewed and holds a little more firmly without breaking the thread, especially when the garment is to be worn by an active person.

Hold the two edges with right sides together. Using the same yarn that was used for the garment and a crochet hook of the appropriate size, join them with slip-stitch as follows: Insert the hook through a st in one side of the seam, *one st in from the edge,* and then through the corresponding st in the matching piece on the other side. You must always work into the corresponding rows of knitting on each piece. Catch the yarn with the hook, draw it through the two pieces, and *straight through the loop on the hook.* Repeat this process on the entire length of seam, working into each row of knitting as you go.

All *side seams* (underarm to waist, sleeves, etc.) should be made in this manner but, unless there is a very good and special reason for doing otherwise, work all of these seams *from the bottom edge to the top edge;* always work *up to, not down to* a given point in the work. For instance, work from the ribbing at the lower edge of the sweater, to the armhole. All *bound-off* seams (tops of shoulder shapings, etc.) should be grafted (Tip ♯65) , unless a cable, rib stitch or some similar pattern has been used. With a simple pullover or cardigan, proceed as follows:

Graft the shoulder seams. Slip-stitch the underarm seams. If there is to be a neckband, or front border to be made (Tip ♯66) , now is the time to work these, as the garment is easier to handle without the added weight of the sleeves. Then, slip-stitch the sleeve seams and, without breaking the yarn, set in the sleeves following these steps: Turn the sleeve right-side out, body wrong-side out, and put the sleeve in the armhole. Pin the center top of the sleeve to the shoulder seam, right sides together. With the *body side* of the sweater facing you, pin from the underarm toward the shoulder seam, easing in any fullness of the sleeve equally along the line as it occurs. Pin the other side to match.

Then, with the *body side* still facing you, work a seam in slip-stitch all around as on other straight seams but, after the decreases have been passed on the armhole shaping, follow the straight line of knitting from this point to the matching point on the other side of the armhole. This insures a very smooth straight seam as the rows of the knitting at the armhole edges serve as a guide. Work into each row of knitting as you go, as the armhole may draw too tightly if more space between sts is allowed.

(65)   GRAFTING

Horizontal: When two bound-off edges need to be joined, *grafting* the seam provides a neater-looking seam than joining with slip-stitch as on side-seams. This grafting looks like another row of knitting, especially when joining two pieces of Stockinette Stitch (Fig. 23). Thread a tapestry needle with matching yarn. With the right side of both pieces facing you, hold the two pieces together with the edges touching. When you observe both pieces carefully, you can see that, on the side farthest away from you there are *chains going away from you* and, on the side nearest you, there are *chains coming toward you.* Each chain is a separate st (Fig. 24). Fasten the thread at the right-hand edge and insert the needle under the first chain coming toward you on the near side, just below the bound-off sts. The needle should be inserted *horizontally, from right to left,* and the yarn drawn through. Then, insert the needle under the matching chain *going away from you* on the opposite side, in the same manner (from right to left, horizontally) and draw the yarn through. On succeeding sts, the needle is inserted into the same place where the yarn was withdrawn on the previous st. The needle and yarn are *always* drawn under each chain, *from right to left, horizontally.*

Not *all* shoulder seams need to be grafted. There *is* a means of grafting pattern stitches, but it is an involved process, and not necessary. Since ribbed or cable-stitch patterns are difficult to match by this means, and are also inclined to have more stretch, it is much wiser to slip-stitch the seam *firmly* so that the shoulder line will not sag.

Vertical Grafting: Although we do not advise grafting side seams,

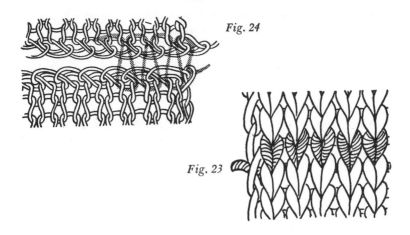

Fig. 24

Fig. 23

there are many other reasons for grafting when joining one piece to another in a vertical position, such as attaching a band of ribbing to the front of a cardigan. It is worked in virtually the same manner as horizontal grafting, *using rows of knitting as a guide,* rather than sts as in Fig. 23. When the rows of knitting match in number, the procedure is as follows: With both right sides of the knitting facing you, hold the two pieces together, with bottom edges at your right and edges touching. With a long piece of work, it is advisable to pin one piece to the other. Thread a tapestry needle with matching yarn and fasten it at the right-hand edge. Insert the needle into one st on the far side and take it under *two rows* of knitting, *at least two threads in* from the edge. As in horizontal grafting, the needle should be inserted *horizontally, from right to left,* and the yarn drawn through. Then, insert the needle under the two matching rows of knitting on the near side (from right to left, horizontally) and draw the yarn through (Fig. 25). Again, as in horizontal grafting, the needle is inserted into the same row of knitting where the yarn was withdrawn on the previous st. This procedure is followed along the entire length of the seam.

FRONT BORDERS FOR CARDIGANS (66)

There are various ways to finish the fronts of a cardigan, and these are usually outlined in any given instruction. But, if you want to

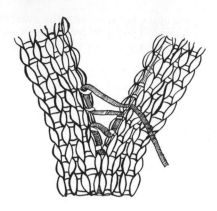

Fig. 25

plan your own cardigan, here are three different methods of finishing which are the most universally approved:

1. *Knitted Ribbing* *(Vertical)* : At least one inch of ribbing at the front edge is retained on a stitch holder after the waistband has been completed. This ribbing has usually been made with a smaller size of needle than the body, and the sts are placed on the holder so that they can be worked later with the same needle. If the neckline is ribbed, this front band should be finished before making the neckband. The sts are ribbed on the smaller needle to form the front band and the buttonholes worked into one of the fronts. It is wise to make the *button* side first so that the buttonholes on the other band can be evenly spaced. However, if you prefer, the buttonholes may be made by machine after the ribbon has been applied. In either case, the sts are transferred from the holder to the smaller needle which was used for the ribbing and worked in the same ribbing for the required length of the front to the neckline. BUT—and here is the difference between a passable job and a very good one—*the border is made slightly shorter* than the front, and you should *always add a st at the inside edge of this border* to make a better seam when grafting. In other words, pick up an extra st at the inside edge of these "held" sts before working the required length, making sure to work this added st in the same type of ribbing. The border is then worked, not to the exact length of the front edge, but at least ¾ inch to 1 inch shorter, to keep the front edge of the cardigan from drooping. This band is then applied with Vertical Grafting (Tip #65), where you may have to "cheat" a little on the border to make it match the

length of the body, because the number of rows may not be the same; so, instead of going under two rows *every* time, go under just one row of the border piece every now and again to make the two pieces come out even.

When the border pieces have been worked, slip the sts of the *left front* band back onto the holder again, until the neckline is picked up, and break the yarn at the *inside edge*. Do *not* break the yarn of the right-hand band, but use the yarn and the needle to continue on with the next operation—picking up the sts around the neckline. Knit (or purl) 2 sts together at the inside edges of the borders to eliminate the "extra" st. When the left front edge has been reached, work off the sts from the holder (in pattern) and then finish the neckband, together with the two front bands, making sure to make the last buttonhole on the same side as before, if necessary, after the first two or three rows have been completed.

2. *Knitted Ribbing (Horizontal)* : Many a cardigan, especially a jacket of the "Chanel" type, calls for a border, the sts of which are picked up all around both fronts and the neckline in one operation. A circular needle is better equipped to hold all these sts, although it is surprising how many sts a 14-inch needle will accommodate when it has to.

The yarn is fastened at the lower edge of the Right Front and, usually, the smaller size needle is used to pick up the required number of sts along this front to the neckline (see Tip #60) . Count the number of sts and place a ring marker on the needle at this point. Pick up the sts around the neckline to the left front and place another marker on the needle. Pick up the same number of sts down the left front as were counted on the right front. Work in ribbing (or whatever type of stitch designated) , making an increase on both sides of each marker, every other row, to miter these two corners. If necessary, work buttonholes into the appropriate side, following Tip #85.

These same directions should be followed if the cardigan is to have a high, medium or low V neckline, with one exception only. You should place the ring markers on each front edge where the decreases for the V-line begin (hopefully, these have been marked) .

3. *Crocheted Border:* This type of border is preferred by many because it is thicker and stronger than a knitted border and seldom needs a ribbon facing.

When working crochet on a knitted edge, the *correct gauge* is necessary. It is wise to practice on a knitted swatch, made exactly in the same stitch, with the same size needles as were used in the body of the sweater, before proceeding to work on the garment itself. The choice of hook size is also very important, as the border must lie flat and smooth, neither ruffling nor puckering (Fig. 26).

Fig. 26

With the *right side* of the knitting facing you, work one row of single crochet and *gauge your work* just as in picking up sts in knitting—work a st into each of three rows, and then skip the fourth row. Therefore, start the first st in the first row of knitting, make the second st in the second row of knitting, the third st in the third row of knitting, and skip the fourth row. On each succeeding row, you must ch 1 to turn, and then work into each original st with single crochet. *Always ch 1 to turn,* and start the first st directly above the last st made on the previous row. It is also better to work single crochet *under the two top threads* of the previous row. Just as in a knitted border, it is wise to have the finished border very *slightly tighter* than the knitting. This can be pressed to the correct proportion on the final touching up.

If a cardigan is to be made for a growing child, you can look to the future and make buttonholes in *both sides* (see Tip #85). In this case, overcast the buttonholes of one side and sew the buttons over them. When the child has outgrown it, and another child of the opposite sex can use it to good advantage, simply close the buttonholes on one side and open them on the other.

(67) *CREW NECKLINES*

Many sports and ski sweaters are designed with a crew neckline, which is not shaped at all or has only a very shallow scoop in front.

So that this type of neckline will slip over the head, it must be *several inches wider* than for a round neck, with only about half the usual number of sts bound off for each shoulder.

Instead of a ribbed neckband, a crew neck is finished with a facing. When the shoulders on the back have been bound off, work the remaining sts as follows: Change to smaller size needles and K 1 row on the wrong side for hemline. Starting with a K row and increasing 1 st at each end of the needle on *every row*, work 2 or 3 rows of Stockinette Stitch with the smaller needles, then change to the larger needles and continue increasing as before until the facing is about 2" or 3" deep. Bind off very loosely.

If the front of the neck is unshaped, work the facing same as for back. If there is to be a shallow shaping, pick up 1 st in each st across the neck, then complete the facing same as for the back.

Join the shoulder seams and the increased edges of both facings, turn the facings to wrong side at the hemlines and whip them carefully in place, catching only the purl nubs so that these sts will be invisible from the right side. Tack the seamlines of facings to the shoulder seams.

INSERTING ZIPPERS (68)

There are many places where a zipper is the best means of closing— side opening of a dress or skirt, back of neck opening, fronts of a cardigan, etc. In many instances, instructions will call for an addition of sts at the side seam (dress or skirt), these sts to be turned in to form a facing which will accommodate the zipper with a "blind" placket. Usually, one or two rows of single crochet around the opening or on one edge will suffice; make sure to keep this crochet firm so that it will not stretch the knitting. Then, following the instructions on the package, pin the zipper in place and sew with thread according to directions. We strongly suggest, however, that the edges of the knitting be *fulled slightly onto the zipper* to keep the zipper flat. If knitting is pulled too tight, zipper will buckle. Instead of regular sewing thread, which might cut wool yarn, it is better to use two or three strands of Six Strand Embroidery Floss. This floss is softer in texture and is available in a great range of colors. It may not last quite so long as sewing thread, but at least it won't damage the knitting and can always be replaced if necessary.

If the zipper shows when placket is finished, work another row of crochet on the overlapping edge and tack the ends down. On the front edges of a cardigan or jacket, you may insert an open-end zipper with either a "fly-front" or a plain closing. The directions for each of these usually come with the package. No matter which type you use, the edges of the knitting should be finished with one or two rows of single crochet to pull them into the correct measurement before applying the zipper.

(69) *BLOCKING (Dry)*

In these days of "bulky knits", there is rarely a good reason for a full blocking operation. It usually suffices if the seams are pressed open with a steam iron (leave the ribbing alone, please), and a quick once-over where the knitting may need it. If it is a sweater, we suggest that *just wearing it* once or twice will block it sufficiently. If it is a skirt or dress you want to block, and it is made of fine yarn with small needles, there are two methods which may be used:

1. Lay a very damp, almost wet, "winter sheet" (cotton flannel) on a flat surface large enough to hold the entire garment, protecting whatever is underneath with a piece of heavy plastic. Place the garment on the damp sheet and "mold" it with the hands into the proper proportions, making liberal use of a tape-measure and checking the dimensions to which it has been made. If pins *must* be used, be sure they are rust-proof, use them sparingly, and remove them as soon as you believe the garment will retain its correct shape. Cover the work with another wet cloth and press it down with the hands so that this dampness may penetrate the knitting. Leave these pieces in position until the knitted fabric is *completely* dry, lifting the cover cloth once in a while to reshape the garment if necessary.

2. Follow directions for "Tailored Finishing and Blocking" (Tip #71).

(70) *BLOCKING (Wet)*

If you are a real knitting addict, and either you or the man of the house is a good do-it-yourselfer, you will find that a "blocking screen" will be in almost constant use. This screen is made similar to a window screen, using a heavy grade of copper or aluminum wire window screening, and wood which is substantial enough to hold the wire taut. The size is up to you, but it should be large enough to block two or more pieces simultaneously. (If many sweaters are being worn by the family, it is almost certain that you would never wash just one at a time!). It should also be made so that the wood pieces will raise the screening *at least* two inches from a flat surface, and be braced at the center to prevent any chance of sagging. It is wise to give the metal parts two or three coats of fine grade enamel to prevent any "bleeding" of the metal. If you are lucky enough to possess a couple of saw-horses, good! Put it on these.

When blocking on the screen, cover it with a heavy piece of cotton flannel. Remove as much moisture as possible from the garment and block according to directions (Tip #69). For faster drying, place an oscillating fan so that it will face directly toward the side edge of the screen and keep the air circulating under and over the cloth and the knitting. Absolutely *no* blocking or drying should be done out of doors unless it is done in *total shade*. The sun's rays can penetrate a cotton cover and bleach colors. If *white wool* has been used, *it will not bleach;* it will turn an ugly tan! Even as you and I, wool will sunburn!

TAILORED FINISHING AND BLOCKING (71)

When assembling, finishing and blocking any fitted garment—blouse, dress, skirt or suit—the following methods are advised for the best results. These methods are not difficult, but they *are* painstaking, and may seem rather complicated at first glance. If you want a first-class result, however, it might be well to remember that you have put in quite a bit of time in its making, not to mention the cost of the material. Nothing is quite comparable to the pride you will have when you wear the beautifully fitted result. A basic knowledge of dressmaking is desirable, but not imperative.

First: Block each piece, separately, by pinning it to a piece of heavy unglazed wrapping paper which has been cut to the proper shape of the *finished* dimensions of that piece. Better still, use unbleached muslin or some similar material, and cut each piece to its required dimensions. Baste the pieces to their muslin counterparts, *right side down,* and dampen the cloth very thoroughly. Press each piece to the proportions of the cloth, with a dry iron, but do not allow the iron to bear down heavily; just enough to make the knitting assume its correct shape and size. (If paper has been used, cover the piece to be blocked with a very damp piece of cloth and press as above.) Remove paper or cloth and allow the knitting to remain in place until all dampness has dispersed. Then, baste the back to the front (s) at the shoulder and side seams (again, with yarn) and try on, *wrong side out.* Any necessary adjustments (tucks, shirrings, darts, etc.) should be made at this time. Pin in these adjustments, take off the garment, and work them in with running back-stitch or slip-stitch crochet, following the fitting lines and making sure that the stitches do not bind. If a shoulder-seam adjustment is necessary (this is usually the crucial point in any fitting operation), make this notation *right now* and either loosen or tighten it as necessary. *Loosening* may be done by un-doing the bind-off and rebinding with a larger needle. *Tightening* may be accomplished by— 1) un-doing the bind-off and re-binding with a smaller needle. 2) crocheting the seam together, pulling it in as much as necessary. 3) reinforcing the entire shoulder seam with seam binding or ribbon (See Page 59).

Next, baste sleeve seams and set into armhole, leaving about six inches open at top of sleeve, three inches each side of shoulder seams. Try on again and pin this portion in, easing it into the remaining part of the armhole. Remove, baste, then join seams, following Tip #64.

If hems are used, all side seams should be joined and pressed open before turning them under. Baste the hems *first* at the turning edge and then at the hemming edge. (Leave *this* basting in until the last final pressing.) *Following one row of knitting* on the wrong side, whip into position, using the same yarn if it is smooth, but, if it is too heavy or nubby, use Six Strand Floss as suggested in Tip #68. When hemming, insert the sewing needle into *just a part of the stitch* at the back so that it will not show through to the front of the work.

It is rarely advisable to stitch any part of knitting by machine. In the first place, it is seldom necessary, as smooth yarns may be purchased in small amounts (wound expressly for making Argyle patterns) in light or heavy (4-ply) weights, and in a great variety of shades and colors. Also, if you are lucky enough to find an outlet for "crewel" yarns, these are extremely strong and the color range is very wide. In the second place, it is almost impossible to join two pieces together by machine-stitching without deviating from the rows or stitches of the knitting; sewing by hand or crocheting with slip-stitch holds just as well and results in much straighter and smoother seams.

Machine stitching *may* be used in the following instances: When applying ribbon or elastic at the waistline of a skirt, it serves a most useful purpose. Again, try the garment on, wrong side out, and pin the ribbon or elastic (one inch wide *at least*) to the waistline, making any necessary adjustments. Baste this to the top of the skirt, allowing no more than one-quarter inch at the top edge to project above it. If elastic is to be used, it is suggested that you use a fairly close stitch-setting and pull the work *and* the elastic as you sew, having the bobbin-thread the same color as the yarn and the top thread the color of the elastic. Stitch three rows—top and bottom edge, and at the center. If you are fortunate enough to have a zig-zag attachment, work in the same manner, using a medium-wide setting for the top and a wide setting at the center. Sew from the inside, with the elastic side up.

This is one of the very few ways of finishing the top of a skirt which will not "roll out", showing the elastic and the zig-zag crocheted casing which holds it in place. It may also be safely worn *over* a blouse to hold it in place.

When the jacket or blouse is finished and you feel that the shoulders do not "set" just right, or you think they may need re-inforcing to keep their original fit, use bias binding or seam binding and apply as follows: Establish the distance you must have between the shoulders *at the back* and cut a piece of tape or binding, allowing a little for turning in the ends. Pin this across one shoulder, the back of the neck (just below any finishing at the neckline) and across the other shoulder—*but—do not ease in* the knitting to the binding for *at least one inch in* from the top of the sleeve. Along the intermediate distance, ease the knitting to the tape by pinning, and then whip it into position at both edges. All too often it is obvious that tape has been used incorrectly when the top of the sleeve forms a sharp little peak at the shoulder, caused by the tape pulling up the top of the sleeve.

If buttonholes have been made in the knitting and there is no knitted facing, it is advisable to face both the button and buttonhole sides with ribbon. Far too seldom, however, is it possible to find the correct color of ribbon which is wide enough to accommodate a button over three-quarters of an inch in diameter. Ribbon which is only one inch wide is practically useless if you wish to make a *horizontal buttonhole* for any button larger than one-half inch wide. It is better to omit buttonholes in the knitting, apply the ribbon, and then have the buttonholes made *vertically* by machine. If you are lucky enough to find the correct width and wish to make them yourself, follow this procedure: pin the ribbon to the *button* side to fit, making sure that the front edge does not sag and allowing enough to turn under at the two ends. Cut this piece and then cut another exactly the same length for the other side. Baste the two pieces into position, try on to make sure they fit, then whip the *button side* ribbon on. Then, *and only then,* pin the two fronts together and mark the position of the buttonholes *on the ribbon.* Remove this ribbon and work the buttonholes in the ribbon to desired size with machine stitching or hand-buttonholing. Cut the holes and overcast them to the knitted buttonholes, making the stitches as unnoticeable as possible. Then, whip the ribbon edges into position.

If a skirt is made in separate panels, it is put together and blocked the same as any other part of the garment. If it is to have an opening at the side, it is finished exactly the same as you would for a skirt of woven material, using snaps, hooks and eyes or a zipper. If it has no opening, follow the directions below for a skirt made on a circular needle. Just make sure to press all seams open.

Skirt Made on Circular Needle. (Note: If skirt is to have elastic at the waist, do not apply until after the work is blocked.) Finish the top of the skirt with single crochet and the lower edge too, if necessary. If the skirt is to be *Wet Blocked,* follow the instructions in Tip #70, using the blocking screen if possible for faster drying. Shape the skirt, using the tape measure very liberally to make it conform to your measurements as outlined in Tip #18. *Do not allow any curving at the side edges* if it can be avoided. You should establish the hipline measurement *at least three inches above* where that measurement was taken, and then continue to taper to the lower edge.

Allow the work to dry partially, then turn and replace it with the side edges at the center. Frequent turning, before it is entirely dry, will discourage any sharp fold lines in the skirt. When thoroughly dry, turn work wrong side out and press out any fold lines or wrinkles with a steam iron.

The above method may be followed for *Dry Blocking,* using a wet cloth underneath and on top of the knitting. As above, turn the work frequently to avoid creasing as much as possible.

When storing *any* knitted garment, make very liberal use of tissue paper inside seams or folding points. The best way to store a skirt is to put several layers of slightly crushed tissue paper inside and *roll* the skirt *lengthwise* to form a tube. If your storage place is not long enough to hold the full length, put some more tissue along the length of this tube and fold it in half. *Never* hang a skirt or a dress, even if it has been lined, and seldom a sweater. When traveling, the same folding method should also be used for packing knitted garments in a suitcase; just a few hard shakes will remove most folds or wrinkles.

WASHING

There is a host of laundering agents on the market that are manufactured for the sole purpose of washing fine woolens. It is strongly
urged that one of these special kinds be used. Nearly all of them give
strict instructions on their use but, if they do not, you should proceed
as follows: if you are going to use a *powdered* product, dissolve the
necessary amount in a separate pan of *hot* water *and make very sure
it is thoroughly dissolved.* Then pour this into the washing receptacle
and cool it down to the correct temperature—tepid or cool, *never hot.*
Squeeze the water through and through the article, *being very careful
not to rub or twist the knitting!* Shrinking or felting is almost certain
to occur if this rule is not followed to the letter.

If the garment is badly soiled, it is better to wash it two or even
three times, in the same amount of cleanser each time, than to use a
large amount just once. More soil can be removed safely and surely,
and the dirt all rinsed out, by using this method. If there are any
small spots, note where they are before putting the garment into the
bath. When it is thoroughly wet, dip a finger-tip into the powder or
liquid and rub this on the spots. Rinse once to see whether they have
been loosened. If they have disappeared, good! If they haven't, quite,
repeat the process. Then, go ahead with the total washing operation.

It is not necessary to use cold water unless there are colors which
might run into each other. Even then, proper washing and *drying*
will prevent bleeding of colors unless, of course, the yarn is of an in-
ferior grade. Tepid or warm water is quite acceptable, but, again,
never hot.

NEVER, under any circumstances, hold garment up while wet.
The weight of the water will stretch the yarn. Press out as much
water as you possibly can while it is still in the basin and then, sup-
porting it carefully with the hands, transfer it to a terry-cloth towel
large enough to fold all around it. Press out some more wetness and
put it into a second towel. Lay it flat on this towel, folding the edges
over it. Roll this lengthwise and wring it *hard.* The garment will not
be harmed, as you are putting all of the stress on the cloth, not the
knitting. Put to dry as in "Wet Blocking" (Tip #70) .

FABRIC SOFTENERS

The new fabric softeners are a boon to knitters. If used in the final
rinse water, yarns, especially those of soft wool or mohair will retain

their softness and fluffiness. They are especially advised for softening orlons and other artificial fibers which are very apt to get "boardy" after a few washings. They also remove static electricity. Make sure, however, that the softener *does not contain bleach! Any chlorine bleach, in particular, will damage white wool* almost beyond repair.

(74)   *REMOVING EXCESS MOISTURE*

There are several good ways to remove moisture: If you have a washing machine with a wringer, wrap the garment (*watch out for those buttons*) in a towel to cover it completely and run it through the wringer once or twice, loosening the mechanism slightly so that the knitting is not damaged. Or, place the knitted piece in a large-mesh bag or old pillow slip. Set the washing machine spinner to *slow* and spin the moisture out; *not dry,* but damp enough to handle when blocking. *Never put it into the dryer.* But, if you don't happen to possess any of these conveniences, and you do have a salad basket (even a plastic colander will do), wrap the knitting in a cloth, loosely, and put it in the basket. Take it outdoors and twirl it around your head to whisk away the extra wetness. You may devise some other means for yourself, but remember this; *too much moisture left in the wool after washing can cause shrinkage.*

(75)   *LENGTHWISE STRETCH*

Any garment or article which is made up mostly of Garter, Seed or some similar stitch which requires *knitting* on each row of the work, will be much more apt to stretch *lengthwise,* because of the nature of the stitch. This should be allowed for in the knitting and measuring, but even so, it is wise to be aware of it when washing, so that you will be prepared to *push it together* when blocking.

(76)   *PROFESSIONAL TOUCHES*

Any garment which has a front (or other) closing, such as a cardigan or jacket, should have the closing on both edges basted together *with yarn, never with thread.* If there are buttons and buttonholes, unfasten the buttons after basting and very lightly whip the buttonholes together before washing and drying. Also, if there are pockets, baste them closed. When dry, these edges will not have stretched nor the buttonholes or pockets become loose and out of shape.

shortened by this method, but you are in real trouble if you try to lengthen it, as every st will be a half stitch off pattern.

TIGHTENING A VERTICAL EDGE (84)

Many coats and jackets require a turned-back hem or facing; some are knitted in, others worked separately to be applied later. In either case, the front edge is almost certain to droop without the following bit of finishing: after the facing is turned back and pressed, work one row of slip-stitch crochet on the right side of the work, just one st in from the very edge, skipping a row of knitting every so often to pull it into correct position. It may also be wise to insert a narrow piece of nylon net as an interfacing, tacking it invisibly to the facing.

MAKING NEAT BUTTONHOLES (85)

Nearly every knitter *hates* to make buttonholes. If you find this a troublesome chore with disappointing results, follow these three steps: Row 1—Bind off the required number of sts at the proper spot *using a smaller size needle,* and finish the row with the regular size needles. Row 2—Work back to the bound-off sts. Turn the work completely around and, using the two-needle method (Tip #28) *and with the smaller needles,* cast on the same number of sts as were bound off, *plus one more st.* Slip the first st from the right-hand needle to the left-hand needle, and pull the extra cast-on st over this st, snugging it up tightly. Turn work around again and finish the row with the regular size needles. Row 3—Work the sts to the *first st which was*

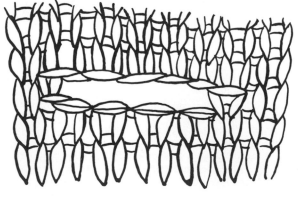

Fig. 27

65

(86)   *cast on.* Then, as in Tip #28, knit into the *back* of this loose st to pull it tight and also into the back of the next st just for good measure (Fig. 27). If making buttonholes into ribbing, however, it is not necessary to use the smaller size needles for the bind-off or cast-on.

ALTERNATIVE METHOD

Another way to make neat buttonholes is to omit them when knitting and make them later. This method is particularly valuable if you are uncertain about the correct placement of the buttons. Try on the garment and mark the position of the buttonholes. Clip a st at the center, loosen the sts on both sides and secure the loops by overcasting each of the two edges with yarn.

(87)   ### POCKET SLITS

It is awkward to finish a pocket welt during the progress of the knitting. To avoid this, work as follows: Work the number of sts from the edge to the start of the pocket. Drop the yarn and, using another piece of yarn *of a sharply contrasting color,* knit the pocket sts. Slip these sts back onto the left-hand needle, pick up the main-color yarn and knit these contrasting sts. When finishing time comes, pull out the contrasting yarn, picking up the sts on two needles, one for the top edge and one for the bottom edge. The welt is worked on the bottom edge in any desired stitch—but—pick up an extra st at each end and work it along with the pattern. Just as in Vertical Grafting (Tip #65), this extra st is the one which is whipped into position. The sts on the other needle may be worked down as a pocket lining, or bound off and have a cloth pocket attached. The same process may be used to make a large buttonhole or any division of work which you would prefer to finish later.

(88)   ### KNITTED BIAS BINDINGS

Depending on how you wish to use this type of trim, you should work it in either of two ways: To bind an edge where the two ends will be joined—work as follows: Cast on the number of sts to form the desired folded width. Then, work the desired length by *increasing one st at the beginning, and decreasing one st at the end of every other row.* (Note: Always work the piece a little short, as bias knitting, like cloth cut on the bias, will stretch considerably.) If the binding is not to be joined—cast on 3 sts. Inc. 1 st at the beginning of every row until you reach the desired width. Then, continue as above to the correct length. Dec. 1 st at the end of every row until 3 sts remain. Bind off. Steam-press thoroughly, and then apply to the edge just as you would apply any bias cloth binding. One thing to remember, however; start the application at the *cast-on edge* so that, if it is a little too long or too short, you can add on or take rows off at the bound-off edge. Since it is often difficult to find a piece of cloth binding of the correct color or shade to use to re-inforce the shoulder seams, you can use a length of this bias knitting instead (Tip #71).

SHORTENING A SLEEVE CAP (89)

Occasionally, because of improper planning, a sleeve will not "set in" the armhole without puckering or sagging, because the sleeve cap is too long from the first bind-off at the underarm to the last bind-off at the top.

Undo the armhole seam, raise the top of the cap, and pin it so that it fits. Mark the outline and count the excess rows. Mark the same outline on the other sleeve. Rip one sleeve cap back to where it needs re-shaping and plan to decrease more rapidly so that the extra rows will be eliminated. Count the number of sts you now have on the needle and mark this number in your notebook. As you re-knit, mark each decrease in the notebook and check the shaping against the outline on the other sleeve. Your notes will serve to shape the second sleeve cap, so that they will both be identical.

Of course, it is possible that the sleeves were too wide for the size of the armhole. In that case, bind off more sts at the underarm before you start to shape the cap. Later, you can take in the sleeve seam to fit properly.

FOR A SNUG WAISTLINE (90)

When knitting a shaped blouse, you may wish to have the waistline fit snugly. Work to within one inch of the exact waistline, then change to smaller needles. Continue to work with these needles for 2″ and then change back to the regular size for the remainder of the work.

If you need more fullness in the front of a fitted blouse than is suggested in the pattern, work as follows: After shaping the waistline on smaller needles, work one-third of the distance across, increase in each st of the next inch of sts, work to the corresponding distance from the opposite edge, increase again in each st of the inch at that point, and finish the row. This extra fullness may be taken in when shaping the neckline.

(91) FOLLOWING INSTRUCTIONS CORRECTLY

INSTRUCTIONS ARE *NOT* WRITTEN TO BE READ: THEY ARE WRITTEN TO BE FOLLOWED. Too many times the knitter will read the entire knitting instructions from start to finish, absorbing little and confusing much. Read them through quickly if you wish, just to see what might happen, and then—when knitting—work each step as it presents itself. *Do not anticipate any step* in the directions until the one before it has been completed.

Because of the high cost of production, instruction books *must* keep the printing to a minimum, and all writing condensed as much as possible. To make these directions more intelligible and easier to follow, break the paragraphs down into small parts by writing each sentence, separately, on a large sheet of paper; use a typewriter if you have one, and leave a double space between each knitting sequence. In this manner, every small step in the directions is seen in its entirety, is more easily understood and much less confusing to follow. When one step has been concluded, cross it out and continue to the next one.

(92) DIFFICULT PATTERN STITCHES

If a pattern stitch involves many rows, break it down in the same manner as above, by writing each row separately on a file card. If many cards are used, number each row to each card and keep them together with an elastic band. When one row is finished, turn to the next card, keeping the cards in the correct sequence for resuming work at a later time.

(93) KNIT A SURPRISE GIFT

If you wish to knit a sweater for a friend as a surprise and don't want to let the cat out of the bag, try to get a friend of the friend to "borrow" a sweater which fits her or him. Take the measurements across the back at the underarm (multiply by 2 for the bust or chest size) —sleeve length at underarm—length from underarm to bottom edge—width of shoulders at the back. This will give you a very good idea of how to compute your knitting.

MAKE AN ENSEMBLE (94)

Thinking of making a new silk or cotton print dress? Why not make a cardigan or jacket of matching or contrasting yarn and line it with the same dress material?

NEEDLE CASES (95)

Save those tubes from paper toweling and aluminum foil! The paper towel tubes are large enough to carry several pairs of 10" needles. The long aluminum-foil tubes will carry 14" needles. When you go to a knitting shop, you never know which size needles you are going to need. You will be prepared to make a swatch for almost anything if you have several sizes to choose from, right at hand. These tubes also make excellent storage containers. Staple the bottom end closed so that the needles will not slip through. Cover the top with tough plastic and secure with an elastic band. Also, keep a file card with the sizes and types of needles you own. Prevents duplication!

SHOULDER PADS (96)

The setting of the shoulder line in a jacket or cardigan may be improved by inserting a thin shoulder pad. A knitted pad is extremely simple to make, and is far better than one you can buy. Simply knit a 4" square of the same yarn in Garter Stitch, fold it into a triangle, and there you are! If you wish it to be a little thicker, insert a few folds of permanent organdy. Tack in place.

SKIRT LININGS (97)

Did you know that you can buy ready-made linings for skirts? They are wonderful for knit-wear!

BOTHERED BY "PILLING"? (98)

Do you find that "pilling" (little wads of wool on the surface) is a problem with fine knits? Wrap your hand with sticky tape, wrong side out, and use it to brush off the pills. This will also brush off lint.

GROSGRAIN RIBBON (99)

Always wash and press all grosgrain ribbon before measuring and cutting. You will find that it almost invariably shrinks in length. Grosgrain ribbon can also be pressed to fit around a curve by stretching out one edge!

(100) *ANGORA*

To help that lovely Angora stole to fluff up before wearing, put it in your refrigerator or freezer for about thirty minutes. Then, put it on the bed and spray it very lightly with clear hair-spray to keep it from shedding. This works with mohair, too.

(101) *KNITTING WITH RIBBON*

There are many kinds and textures of ribbons and about as many ways to work with them. They may be used alone or worked with yarns (see Tip #5) . The methods used depend entirely upon the type of garment you wish to make.

Ribbons are manufactured from many different kinds of materials —rayon, silk, nylon, etc., and combinations of these. Some are crisp, made of taffeta or organdy; others are very soft and pliable and made of pure silk or silk-and-rayon mixture; some are woven or printed to give a tweed effect, and still others have metallic threads incorporated in the edges or center. There are "fuse-cut" ribbons and woven ribbons. All have their own particular uses, and these are defined in the instruction books which have designs made especially to suit the texture of the ribbon and the style of the particular garment to be made. In every case, the stitch to be used is outlined and should be very carefully followed and learned. As in all the preceding tips, *learn the method of making the stitch first,* get the *gauge* required in the directions and, using the rules for measurement (Tip #16) , follow all instructions very carefully.

The following are ways to work with ribbon which may be of interest to those who like to "play around" with different methods and results. If the results are desirable, and you would prefer to use one of these as against the one suggested in the pattern book, *make sure once again to obtain the correct* GAUGE specified in the instruction for the particular garment you wish to make.

1. Keeping ribbon flat, wind it around the needle, inserting the needle into the *back* of the sts on the knit rows, and purling in the regular manner on the purled rows.

2. A braided effect may be obtained by using the same method with

one exception only. After inserting the needle into the st on the knit row (into *back* of st), instead of bringing ribbon toward you *under* the needle and then away, bring the ribbon toward you *over* the needle and then away from you under the needle.

3. The following method of using ribbon produces the woven effect illustrated (Fig. 28). It requires time and a great deal of patience to learn, but it can result in a really beautiful garment. When prop-

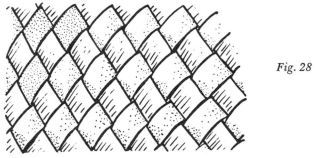

Fig. 28

erly executed, this stitch will produce a flat, diagonal weave with no holes appearing in the finished material; it also has less stretch than most other methods.

Great care must be exercised in keeping the ribbon flat when winding on the needle. It is suggested that a mark be made along one surface of the ribbon for a considerable length. This will facilitate the keeping of this marked surface against the surface of the needle, thus eliminating the chance of the ribbon's being twisted while being worked.

Before starting, practice winding the ribbon around the needle, spirally, several times. You will notice that it is necessary to drop the ribbon after each turn around the needle. As in this practice winding, so you will have to drop the ribbon after each st, to readjust it for the next st, making sure that the ribbon comes out of that st *flat* (Fig. 29). On the purled row, the ribbon must be wound around the needle in the opposite manner from that in regular purling. As in knitting, keep the ribbon flat and readjust it after the completion of each st. Wind it *under* the needle *away* from you, and then *over* the needle *toward* you. Always work loosely, and *do not pull back on the ribbon.* If you are in the habit of winding *yarn* around any of your fingers, or holding it tightly, *you must not do so* in working with ribbon in this manner.

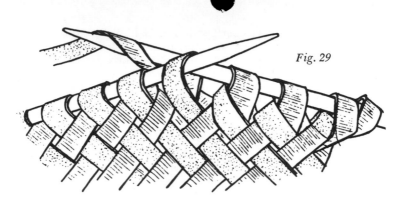

Fig. 29

Always pull out several yards of ribbon ahead of your knitting. In working any ribbon stitch, the ribbon will twist from the work to the spool. Pin the ribbon to the spool and hold it up to allow untwisting. When working the flat stitch given in Method #3, the ribbon will twist one way going across the row and untwist itself on the return row. You will find that it will be less bothersome if you work to the center of the piece and then let the ribbon untwist at this point.

Clothing made with ribbon, in *any* type of stitch, must be just as carefully worked to gauge as that made of yarn. In working this *flat* ribbon stitch in particular, you must make sure that the knitting is kept flat and that the correct *gauge* is obtained. The difference of half a st in an inch is of the greatest importance, as there are so few sts to an inch in the gauge.

Following Tip #23, make a large swatch and bind off. Put this swatch right side down on a well-padded pressing board and cover it with a damp cloth. Set your iron to "silk" control and press. Remove the cloth, turn to "synthetic" control, turn off the steam and press until thoroughly dry. Remove from the pressing board and *then* check your gauge for sts and rows per inch.

To Finish Ribbon Garments. As in Tip #71, the finishing of a knitted garment requires a basic knowledge of dressmaking. Each piece must be thoroughly pressed before basting and sewing. The garment must be basted and fitted *first,* then the seams machine- or hand-stitched together, the material being treated exactly as though it were dress material. Finishing of open edges such as bottoms of skirt, blouse, sleeves, and necklines, may be worked in single crochet, just as in yarn knitting. These points, and all finishing points such as seam allowances, darts, edges, etc., should be pressed as the final touch.

PLAIN SOCKS (102)

MATERIALS:

3 oz. of 3-ply yarn
1 set of 7-inch DP Knitting Needles, size 2

GAUGE: 7½ sts = 1 inch

To Begin. With ♯2 needles, cast on 64 sts *loosely*—20 sts on first needle, 20 sts on 2nd needle and 24 sts on 3rd needle. Join carefully, making sure not to twist sts on needles, and work round and round in K 2, P 2 ribbing for 3". Then, work in Stockinette Stitch (K all sts in each round) for 7" or until piece measures the desired length to top of heel.

To Make Heel. Slip the sts from one needle to the other until you have 32 sts on one needle and 16 sts on each of the other two. The 32 sts on the one needle are to be worked for the heel. Proceed as follows:

Row 1 — * K 1 st, Sl 1 st—rep from * across the row to the last 2 sts. K these 2 sts.
Row 2 — P all sts.
Repeat these two rows for 2½" and end on a K row; i.e., finish the K row.

To Turn Heel. P 18 sts, P 2 tog, P 1 and turn knitting around so that the right side of the work is facing you. There will be sts left at the end of the needle but, *ignoring these,* use this same needle for the next row. Then, sl the first st, K 5, SKP and K 1. Turn work as before. Sl the first st and P to the st in front of the gap made by turning on the previous row. P these 2 sts (one on either side of the gap) together, P 1 st more and turn. Continue in this manner, always slipping the first st after turning and working to the gap, decreasing the 2 sts either side of the gap, plus knitting or purling 1 more st. There will be 18 sts left when all sts at the sides of the needles are used up, and you will end on a K row.

To Make Gusset. Combine all 32 sts on the two instep needles onto one needle. Then, on the heel you have just finished, slip the first 9 sts off onto one needle and, using the yarn at end of *last* 9 sts on original heel needle, knit up 18 sts along the side of heel (see Tip #59). Make sure the sts are evenly spaced between the heel and instep and make the last st right up close to the instep sts.

Use another needle to work across the 32 instep sts, and still another needle to pick up 18 sts along other side of heel. With this same needle, K the 9 sts from the first heel needle. Thus you have 27 sts on each of the two heel needles, and 32 sts on the instep needle.

To Decrease For Gusset. Number your needles as follows:
#1 needle going from the instep to the back of heel—27 sts.
#2 needle going from the back of heel to instep—27 sts.
#3 needle going across instep—32 sts.
Round 1—#1 needle—K 1, SKP, K to end.
           #2 needle—K to last 3 sts, K 2 tog, K 1.
           #3 needle—K all sts.
Round 2—K all sts on all three needles.

Repeat these two rounds until there are 16 sts on #1 and #2 needles, and 64 sts in all. Work round and round until the sock measures, from the very back of the heel, 1½″ less than the desired length (or size) of sock.

To Toe Off.
Round 1—#1 needle—K 1, SKP, K to end.
           #2 needle—K to last 3 sts, K 2 tog, K 1.
           #3 needle—K 1, SKP, K to last 3 sts, K 2 tog, K 1.
Round 2—K all sts on all three needles.

Repeat these two rounds until there are 6 sts on #1 and #2 needles and 12 sts on #3 needle.

To Kitchener Stitch the Toe. Slip all sts on #1 and #2 needles onto one needle and break yarn, leaving about 18″. Thread this yarn into a yarn needle. Hold the two needles together (parallel with each other) with the sts near the right end of needles. Insert needle, *knitwise,* into first st on the front needle and slip this st off. Insert needle *purlwise* into the second st on this same needle and pull the yarn through, leaving *this* st *on* the needle. *Then,* insert needle *purlwise* into first st on back needle and slip it off. Insert needle *knitwise* into the second st on same needle and pull yarn through, leaving *this* st *on* the needle. Continue in this manner until there is one st left on each needle. Pull out your knitting needles, run your hand up through the sock, and tack these 2 sts down to the sts right next to them. Weave thread into the seam made by decreasing, and cut off. Wash and block (see Tip #72).

ARGYLE SOCKS (103)

MATERIALS: 3-ply yarn
  2 oz. Main Color—M
  1 oz. of one Diamond Color—A
  1 oz. of another Diamond Color—B
  15 yds of one Cross Color—C
  15 yds of another Cross Color—D
  1 package of 10 Yarn Bobbins
  1 pr. SP needles, size 2
  1 set of 7-inch DP Needles, size 2
GAUGE: $7\frac{1}{2}$ sts = 1 inch

Before starting work, wind two full bobbins each of the main color (M) and the two diamond colors (A and B) —also two bobbins each of the two cross colors (C and D).

(N.B. Argyle socks *must* be made on two needles, *working back and forth,* as long as there are changes of color being made.)

Cast on 62 sts on the straight needles, *very loosely,* with M. Work in ribbing of K 2, P 2 for 3″ (see Tip #32). Break yarn. The remainder of sock is worked in Stockinette Stitch.

On first row of pattern, following the chart, tie in your first bobbin of A. Leave about 3″ of yarn whenever tying in. After first bobbin has been tied, and first 2 sts worked, tie in remaining eight bobbins (you will use only nine bobbins at any one time) when it comes their turn to be worked, as follows: Hold the new piece of yarn 3″ from end and, using a crochet hook, insert it into back of the st *below* the next st on left-hand needle. Pull a loop of yarn through this bump, then pull the free end of yarn through the loop. This will tie the yarn in securely.

When changing one color for another, always put the yarn you have just finished using, *over* the yarn you are going to use, bringing this new color up from underneath. This will avoid making a hole at the point of change of color.

When tying one color to another, after completion of diamonds, tie the two ends together with a square knot (see Tip #45) right up against the needle, leaving about 3″ of free end, enough to thread a needle later on, to work into back when fastening off at end of work.

For Tall Diamond Pattern, work according to Chart 1 (page 78).

For Flat Diamond Pattern, work according to Chart 2 (page 79).

Heel. Slip off the first 16 sts onto one DP needle, 30 sts onto the second needle, and the last 16 sts onto the third needle. Turn the sts at end of third needle toward the sts at end of first needle, bringing the two outside edges of work together with the right side of the knitting facing you. Slip all 32 sts together on one needle. These make up the heel sts. The remaining 30 sts are to be worked in diamond pattern for the instep, completing one, two or three diamonds for the instep, keeping the continuity of pattern, and before working the heel. Leave these sts on the needle. Break off all colors.

When heel has been completed and turned (see Plain Socks, page 00), using Main Color (M), break yarn and tie in at instep end of heel on the right side of heel, with right side of work facing you. Knit up sts from instep to heel (see Plain Socks), K off all sts on heel needle and K up same number of sts down the other side of heel toward instep, making the last st at the point of the instep. Purl back on all 54 sts. They will be rather crowded for the first few rows, but will ease up as work progresses.

To Decrease For Gusset:

Row 1—K 1, SKP, K to within last 3 sts of end of needle, K 2 tog, K 1.

Row 2—Purl all sts.

Repeat these two rows until 32 sts remain on needle.

Continue working in Stockinette Stitch until side of gusset and foot measures same length as the instep piece, ending with a K row. Then, divide these 32 sts onto two needles (16 sts on each) numbering these needles #1 and #2, this designation to be used later. Join work, knitting every round, until sole of sock measures 1½" less than desired length.

To Toe Off. Follow instructions for toe on plain socks.

To Finish. Graft gusset to instep (see Tip #65). Graft the back seam, using the same color of grafting thread for the color of diamond. DO NOT ATTEMPT TO PULL BACK AN ARGYLE SOCK BY REMOVING NEEDLES. Work it back to point of error, stitch for stitch. Watch carefully on every row to see that it is done correctly, checking with your chart, thus avoiding the necessity of pulling back more than one row.

If you will follow the Argyle chart faithfully, until you KNOW exactly what you are doing, you should have no ripping to do.

CHART 1, FOR TALL ARGYLE DIAMOND SOCKS

ROWS	(A)	(M	C	M	D	M)	(B)	(M	D	M	C	M)	(A)
1 & 2	2	13	1	0	1	13	2	13	1	0	1	13	2
3 & 4	3	11	1	2	1	11	4	11	1	2	1	11	3
5 & 6	4	9	1	4	1	9	6	9	1	4	1	9	4
7 & 8	5	7	1	6	1	7	8	7	1	6	1	7	5
9 & 10	6	6	1	8	1	5	10	5	1	8	1	5	6
11 & 12	7	3	1	10	1	3	12	3	1	10	1	3	7
13 & 14	8	1	1	12	1	1	14	1	1	12	1	1	8
15 & 16	8	0	1	14	1	0	14	0	1	14	1	0	8
	(A	C	A)	(M	(B	D	B	D	B)	(M)	(A	C	A)
17 & 18	7	1	2	12	2	1	12	1	2	12	2	1	7
19 & 20	6	1	4	10	4	1	10	1	4	10	4	1	6
21 & 22	5	1	6	8	6	1	8	1	6	8	6	1	5
23 & 24	4	1	8	6	8	1	6	1	8	6	8	1	4
25 & 26	3	1	10	4	10	1	4	1	10	4	10	1	3
27 &28	2	1	12	2	12	1	2	1	12	2	12	1	2
29 & 30	1	1	14	0	14	1	0	1	14	0	14	1	1

31 & 32	Same as Rows 28 & 27
33 & 34	" " " 26 & 25
35 & 36	" " " 24 & 23
37 & 38	" " " 22 & 21
39 & 40	" " " 20 & 19
41 & 42	" " " 18 & 17
43 & 44	" " " 16 & 15
45 & 46	" " " 14 & 13
47 & 48	" " " 12 & 11
49 & 50	" " " 10 & 9
51 & 52	" " " 8 & 7
53 & 54	" " " 6 & 5
55 & 56	" " " 4 & 3

Row 57 is worked the same as Row 2. Then, on Row 58, break off all A and B bobbins. Substitute B bobbins for A bobbins and substitute one A bobbin for the B bobbin. Then, work Row 3 with these same color changes. Keeping these color changes in mind, and substituting C for D and D for C, continue as follows

ROWS	(B)	(M	D	M	C	M)	(A)	(M	C	M	D	M)	(B)
59 & 60	3	11	1	2	1	11	4	11	1	2	1	11	3
61 & 62	4	9	1	4	1	9	6	9	1	4	1	9	4
63 & 64	5	7	1	6	1	7	8	7	1	6	1	7	5

ETC.

CHART 2, FOR FLAT ARGYLE DIAMOND SOCKS

ROWS	(A)	(M	C	M	D	M)	(B)	(M	D	M	C	M)	(A)
1	2	13	1	0	1	13	2	13	1	0	1	13	2
2	3	11	1	2	1	11	4	11	1	2	1	11	3
3	4	9	1	4	1	9	6	9	1	4	1	9	4
4	5	7	1	6	1	7	8	7	1	6	1	7	5
5	6	5	1	8	1	5	10	5	1	8	1	5	6
6	7	3	1	10	1	3	12	3	1	10	1	3	7
7	8	1	1	12	1	1	14	1	1	12	1	1	8
8	8	0	1	14	1	0	14	0	1	14	1	0	8
	(A	C	A)	(M)	(B	D	B	D	B)	(M)	(A	C	A)
9	7	1	2	12	2	1	12	1	2	12	2	1	7
10	6	1	4	10	4	1	10	1	4	10	4	1	6
11	5	1	6	8	6	1	8	1	6	8	6	1	5
12	4	1	8	6	8	1	6	1	8	6	8	1	4
13	3	1	10	4	10	1	4	1	10	4	10	1	3
14	2	1	12	2	12	1	2	1	12	2	12	1	2
15	1	1	14	0	14	1	0	1	14	0	14	1	1

16	Same as Row 14
17	" " " 13
18	" " " 12
19	" " " 11
20	" " " 10
21	" " " 9
22	" " " 8
23	" " " 7
24	" " " 6
25	" " " 5
26	" " " 4
27	" " " 3
28	" " " 2
29	" " " 1

Break off A and B bobbins. Substitute B bobbins for A bobbins and an A bobbin for the B bobbin.

Substitute C bobbins for D bobbins and D bobbins for C bobbins, without breaking off the yarn, as these colors will cross at this point. Keeping these color changes in mind, continue as follows:

ROWS	(B)	(M	D	M	C	M)	(A)	(M	C	M	D	M)	(B)
30	2	13	1	0	1	13	2	13	1	0	1	13	2
31	3	11	1	2	1	11	4	11	1	2	1	11	3
32	4	9	1	4	1	9	6	9	1	4	1	9	4

ETC.

READER'S NOTES